GO TO
CHURCH

CHANGE
THE WORLD

GO TO
CHURCH
CHANGE
THE WORLD

Christian Community as Calling

Gerald J. Mast

Herald Press

Library of Congress Cataloging-in-Publication Data
Mast, Gerald J., 1965-
    Go to church, change the world : Christian community as calling /
Gerald J. Mast.
        p. cm.
    Includes bibliographical references (p.   ) and indexes.
    ISBN 978-0-8361-9564-4 (pbk. : alk. paper) 1. Church attendance.
2. Christian life—Anabaptist authors. I. Title.
    BV4523.M37 2011
    262—dc23

                                                        2011043162

Unless otherwise noted, Scripture text is quoted, with permission, from
the *New Revised Standard Version*, © 1989, Division of Christian Edu-
cation of the National Council of Churches of Christ in the United
States of America.

GO TO CHURCH, CHANGE THE WORLD
Copyright © 2012 by Herald Press, Harrisonburg, Virginia 22802
    Released simultaneously in Canada by Herald Press,
    Waterloo, Ontario N2L 6H7. All rights reserved.
Library of Congress Control Number: 2011043162
International Standard Book Number: 978-0-8361-9564-4
Printed in United States of America
Cover design by Merrill Miller
Book design by Josh Byler

15 14 13 12 11   10 9 8 7 6 5 4 3 2 1

To order or request information, please call 1-800-245-7894 in the U.S.
or 1-800-631-6535 in Canada. Or visit www.heraldpress.com.

To my children:
Anna Lynn, Jacob Daniel, and Jorian Thomas

CONTENTS

WITNESS: BECOMING PRIESTLY

FOREWORD

In a time when the practice of yielding oneself to others within a real and enduring community is quite beyond the pale of Western experience, Gerald Mast's book title—*Go to Church, Change the World*—strikes the ear as archaic, naïve, and simply weird. Not a few book browsers will hear this title, do the aural equivalent of a double-take, and then say something sophisticated, like, "Wha-?"

A possible second take for this casual browser could be to observe that the *idea* of "go to church, change the world" is potentially interesting (let's leave the *practicing* of this idea out of it for the moment). There's some merit, is there not, in the *idea* of the church that is a "place" where one "goes" and experiences oneself as "belonging," as though one could actually belong; as though our occasional attendance actually constituted "going"; as though "places" were actually still real.

A great deal has been written over the last thirty years about this idea of "place." Place matters, as every twenty-first-century urban planner now opines. Just at the time in human history when "place" has disappeared from our lives, neighborhood and community and soda shop having been plan-fully paved over, "place" has become all the rage.

Mast's casual browser might even, at this point, be wishing that the title of his book were *Walk to Church, Change the World*, as this hipster likely already lives in a neighborhood where one can walk to the micro grocer-franchise to pick up enough fair-trade coffee beans, free-range chicken eggs, and organic arugula to hold one over between lunch out and dinner out.

And speaking of "place," we must all have our "third space" too, mustn't we? Churchless as we now actually are, home and work can't fulfill that need we have for a place where everybody knows our name, or at least our unique "grande-no-whip-low-fat-mocha-extra-shot-extra-hot" coffee order that the check-out girl shouts over to the barista before we even have to say a word.

"Belonging" rocks now also—at least the *idea* of it. This is especially true at our no-name, non-denominational "church community" that used to foolishly over-emphasize "believing." People want to "belong," see, and once they really experience what it feels like to "belong" in a, like, "community" (a walkable one, preferably, with an espresso bar in the narthex), then everything else totally falls into place.

Of course, none of these ideas ever survives nascency. Next year we'll all read that the trend is outdated. "Place" will be so yesterday. There'll be a new, hot book about it, downloadable to our mobile devices. Year after that, we'll need to become letter writers again (how embarrassed we'll feel to still use email or text or Twitter; it'll be *actual* text that reifies our humanity—ink words on real paper delivered by human postmen is where it'll be at!). God knows what comes then. Make it up. It doesn't really matter, because little of this is actually real.

In humiliating relief to what the cultural and intellectual fashionistas are constantly averring as important, Gerald Mast suggests, simply, that, "if we are to live in Jesus-centered truth, we must go to church." Mast goes further than this; not only must we go to church, but we must read the Bible (he means the actual Bible) and undergo baptism and participate in daily and weekly church mundanities like the choir, the committees, and the clean-up crew. When Mast says, "go to church," he means actually going to an actual church with the kind of actual people one is likely to find in such a place, people infuriatingly much like the people we, ourselves, are.

I don't think I've mentioned, yet, how much I love this book! To the modern and postmodern mind alike, Mast's beautiful treatise is close to nonsensical, and so desperately needed. Going to church matters, he shows us, both to the working out of our salvation and to the transformation of the world. The actual practice of yielding ourselves to Christ's actual body, and of doing so incarnationally, just as Jesus yielded himself to his actual body, matters in every way! We must be part of an actual place of gathering, one that stays put day after dreary day, an actual place with actual people in the actual world where actual heartaches and actual problems plague actual relationships every disappointing day.

No wonder we read Mast's title and blurt, "Wha-?" We would rather exercise a more moment-by-moment flexibility to drop in, as interest piques, to "world café" salons where we can ruminate with other ruminants about the importance of things like "place," all the while sipping upon our grande-no-whip-low-fat-mocha-extra-shot-extra-hot drink, pleasantly enveloped within a most vague impersonation of an Italian café from some piazza far, far away.

In his famous prayer in the seventeenth chapter of John, Jesus makes a declaration that is not unlike Mast's: "I gave them the same glory you gave me," Jesus says to his Father, "so they may be one as we are one—I in them and you in me—so that they may be brought to total unity. Then the world will know that you sent me and have loved them even as you have loved me."

Translation: The world will be able to know the most important thing that must be known, through Jesus' body dwelling together in loving unity! John Howard Yoder, in *Body Politics*, said it this way: "The people of God is called to be today what the world is called to be ultimately." Simpler translation still: Go to church, change the world!

Mast walks beautifully through the pages of this book as one moves liturgically through the order of Sunday worship. With him, we consider afresh how it is that going to church, joining the church, giving to the church, and, yes, yielding to the church moves us ever more powerfully into a new and transformational posture with and for the world. Our formation ever more deeply into Christ and the church does not produce an ever increasing irrelevancy to the world. Exactly to the contrary!

There is a mystery here, and Mast captures this mystery both through the direct appeal he makes, and in the elegant—even poetical—structure of it. I was reminded, as I spiraled deeper and at the very same time higher through his treatise, of C.S. Lewis' memorable line from The Last Battle—"farther up and further in." Our concrete usefulness to the changing of the world expands in scale and scope as we concretely give ourselves to the deep work of loving and growing with the people with whom we are covenanted to belong. We can't give what we don't have!

What the world needs is not disembodied *ideas* about love and forgiveness and justice and peace; the world needs our capacity to *be* these things, a capacity that can only be grown in the crucible of covenantal relationships over time.

Meditate on *Go to Church, Change the World* as a personal devotional guide. Draw upon it as a liturgical companion for worship planning. Recommend it as a small group or Sunday School study text. Read it together as a whole church to bring renewal to the life and witness of your congregation. Do all four.

But, first things first. Go to church!

John Stahl-Wert is president of Pittsburgh Leadership Foundation (servingleaders.com), founder of SHIP (theshipcompany. com), and internationally best-selling author of The Serving Leader, Ten Thousand Horses, *and* With: A True Story.

PREFACE AND ACKNOWLEDGMENTS

I began thinking about the meaning of Christian calling when I was a student at a small church-related college. My peers and I worried about what we were called to do with our lives. Influenced by a vision of God's sovereignty, we imagined that God had a plan for each of our lives and that it was our job to find out what it was. We played mind games. If we had certain skills, did that mean God expected us to use them? Or were these skills distractions from the sacrificial discipleship God expected from us?

In that setting, it was a relief to encounter a theology of vocation that affirmed our skills and strengths as gifts to be offered in the service of God's project to redeem the whole world. This perspective, which had become a movement at many evangelical Christian colleges in the 1980s, encouraged us to develop a Christian worldview that would shape the pursuit of our chosen profession.

During that same time, some of my mentors from the Reformed tradition introduced me to the writings of John Howard Yoder, a Mennonite thinker who helped me remember the call I had accepted in baptism. This call was direct and straightforward: will you renounce Satan and all works of darkness and join yourself to Jesus Christ and the church? In the years since, I have realized that by answering "yes" to that question I was at the same time saying "yes" to God's plan to redeem the world. God's redemption is taking place through the body of Jesus Christ presented to the world wherever that peaceful body appears. Our first calling, therefore, is life together in this body of Christ.

I am thankful to my mentors from a variety of Christian backgrounds who helped me to see the simplicity and clarity of the Christian calling. Among these are Kim Phipps, my undergraduate academic advisor at Malone College; Jerry Herbert, of the American Studies Program, who assigned John Howard Yoder; John Stahl-Wert, my wise pastor during graduate school years; and J. Denny Weaver, my Bluffton University mentor and colleague, whose friendship and tireless discussion of Anabaptist theology have been profound gifts to me.

Bluffton University provided the intellectual and professional context for this project in numerous ways. The university awarded me two grants during the summers of 2005 and 2008, making it possible for me to interview people and read books and take notes without breaking the household budget. A fall 2005 sabbatical leave provided focused time for developing early drafts of the chapters. As part of Bluffton's Pathways to Mission and Vocation program, funded by the Lilly Endowment, I was invited to be the faculty scholar during the spring of 2006, which enabled me to share initial chapter drafts with colleagues for feedback and discussion on a monthly basis. Among those colleagues who provided useful and, at times, challenging feedback were Trevor Bechtel, Laura Brenneman, Perry Bush, Larry George, Jeff Gundy, Karen Klassen Harder, Hans Houshower, Jim Harder, George Lehman, Lawrence Matthews, Pam Nath, Hamid Rafizadeh, Alex Sider, Sally Weaver Sommer, Willis Sommer, and Rory Stauber. Although I have not always conformed to the perspectives of my colleagues, the book has been strengthened greatly by the conversations provoked by these and other friends.

Students in my Communication Ethics classes from 2007 to 2011 read drafts of these chapters and provided a student perspective. Two research assistants in the Communication and Theatre Department assisted with the preparation of the manuscript: Anna Yoder and Rachel Giovarelli. Finally, it should be noted that the first four sections of the book reflect Bluffton's enduring values of discovery, respect, community, and service, thereby signifying its roots in the soil of Bluffton University and the church to which it relates: Mennonite Church USA.

I am grateful to the keen editorial eyes of Amy Gingerich and Byron Rempel-Burkholder at Herald Press who helped me focus the vision for the book and revise it for a broader audience. It has been a pleasure to work with the staff at Herald Press whose professionalism and accessibility persists amidst challenging institutional realities.

My wife Carrie read numerous drafts and offered many useful suggestions for simplifying and illustrating my ideas. Her deep commitment to a life of service has inspired me to be more Christ-centered and neighbor-oriented in my daily life. I thank God daily for the extraordinary gift of her love.

During the writing of this book, my children Anna and Jacob grew from energetic toddlers to precocious elementary students. Their lives and love are reflected in the following pages, as is the joy with which our family has welcomed a new member, Jorian Thomas. The book is dedicated to these children of mine, with the prayerful hope that they will discover their calling amidst the life of God's people.

INTRODUCTION

What is the point of my life? While many profound and challenging answers have been proposed to this basic and persistent question, this book offers a simple answer from a radical Christian perspective rooted in the Anabaptist tradition. Jesus Christ calls us to be his ambassadors of peace in a lovely but broken world, and he sends us to join God's great plan to reconcile and restore the whole creation (2 Corinthians 5:19-20).

How do we do this? We do it by letting God's love flow through us to the world, just as Jesus did, offering all our gifts and resources to the work and glory of God. Moreover, we follow this calling by living together with other believers who are also pursuing God's purposes. We join the church of Jesus Christ and stay with it through thick and thin, pouring out our lives with our brothers and sisters in Christ for the love of God and the hope of salvation.

We are called to be the church in the world whether we are choosing a college major, finding our first job, facing a mid-life crisis, or heading into retirement. The call comes to us amidst dramatic life choices as well as during the routines of daily life, in the context of paid or unpaid work. The church is around us in all of its flawed and hopeful forms. The saving and reconciling work of God is unfolding, ready for our involvement. The question is not what we should do but rather whether we will do it.[1] Will we give our lives to Jesus Christ and to the mission of Jesus' body in the world today? Will we do it now and every day? Or will we give ourselves

over to other priorities, such as career advancement, empire-
building or pursuit of an affluent lifestyle?

Come and live

Sometimes, placing our lives and property at the disposal of
Jesus Christ and the church is seen as a hard and demanding calling, one that involves guilt and undermines joy. This
view assumes that Christ calls us to neglect our bodies and the
desires that energize our lives. This book rejects such a view.
Instead, Christ's call, though it involves giving some things
up, leads to liberation and true delight. This might sound
counterintuitive, but it is true.

In a recent issue of *The New York Times*, amidst all the bad
news about the crashing stock-market, the frozen credit, the
700 billion dollar bailout, and the end of the financial world
as we know it, there was an intriguing article entitled: "Are
Bad Times Healthy?"[2] According to the article, from studies
of the Great Depression in the 1930's Dust Bowl to analyses
of the decline of coffee prices in Columbia, researchers agree
that during times of economic decline, people overall tend to
be healthier and live longer. This correlation between reces-
sion and better health seems to apply across cultural contexts,
including both developing and developed nations.

Why would this be? One researcher put it this way: "The
value of time is higher during economic boom times. So people
work more and do less of the things that are good for them,
like cooking at home and exercising; and people experience
more stress due to the rigors of hard work during booms."[3]

In other words, the cost of maintaining a great job, a hefty
stock portfolio, and a big house full of nice things could actually be bad for our health. And losing all of it could be good
for our health. As it turns out, this is confirmed both in the
New York Times and in the Bible.

When Jesus calls us to give up everything to follow after
him, "to come and die," as the great German Lutheran theologian Dietrich Bonhoeffer put it, he is telling us to give it
all up. This is not because he wants us to be miserable but
because it is good for us to live that way. The call is really

to come and live! It is good for our health, for our lifespan, and for our humanity. The life of self-denial, of taking up the cross, of giving up the pursuit of wealth and possessions is in fact the way to eternal life.

For those of us who have absorbed the work-centered and self-fulfilling habits of Western middle-class lifestyles, this call of Jesus Christ is a profound challenge because it places God's will and work, not ours, at the center of our life plans. It invites us to let go of our compulsions to succeed and instead to yield our lives to the triumph that God has already accomplished through Jesus Christ on our behalf. It welcomes us into the church of Jesus Christ and urges on us the adventure of being the church in our daily lives. You may already have answered this call by giving your life to the mission of the church. For you, this book reaffirms vital practices you may have forgotten or taken for granted. Alternatively, you may have responded to the call of Christ in a more abstract form, such as "accepting Jesus Christ" or "believing in Jesus." For you, the practices described in this book can help you make your belief concrete and visible in everyday life.

This book links commonplace practices such as reading the Bible and eating meals together with the good life that Jesus offers. They are not clever strategies for self-fulfillment or heroic sacrifice; neither do they represent cutting-edge theology. They are ordinary yet frequently neglected practices of faith that become extraordinary when we undertake them prayerfully as members of Christ's body. We can expect them to change us, as well as our surrounding world. To understand how such practices of yielding could lead to God-directed transformation, however, we must consider what it means to pray.

Pray without ceasing

A few years ago, following the death of my grandparents, I inherited a small German prayer book entitled *Die ernsthafte Christenpflicht* [*Prayer Book for Earnest Christians*], which had originally belonged to my great-grandmother. Her maiden name was inscribed inside the front cover: "Miss

Elizabeth Hershberger." Since she was married to my great-grandfather Alvin Swartzentruber in 1915 and the date of the book's publication was 1914, I assume she received this as a gift at her baptism—which typically occurs not long before marriage in Amish communities such as hers. Knowing a bit of German, I began reading the prayers in this book, curious about how my great-grandmother and many of my ancestors had been encouraged to understand the meaning of baptism, how they learned to express their hopes and fears and doubts and delights—the prayers of their hearts.

I was immediately intrigued by the book's topics and settings for prayer. There were morning prayers, evening prayers, prayers before meals, prayers after meals, prayers before communion, prayers before a sermon, prayers for sickness, prayers for funerals, prayers for discipleship, prayers for hard times, prayers for political authorities, and prayers for enemies. The prayer book addressed both the ordinary and the extraordinary experiences of life. Those who compiled it understood that all of life—every detail—could be lifted up in prayer, given the attention and care that prayer assumes, and granted the presence of the Creator. Moreover, the compilers assumed that we could learn from the prayers of others—who have already learned how to pray—in order to give expression to our own feelings and our own mindfulness. My grandparents and my great-grandparents had prayed these prayers, which were not at first their own, but which had become their own. In studying these prayers, I learned two important lessons about prayer.

First, gratitude for the gift of life is not only the starting point of prayer, it is a condition that makes possible all Christian living that flows from the Word of God. "O Heavenly Father, you have again let this day dawn. Help us remember that it is your gracious gift."[4] Those basic yet essential words are found in the first morning prayer of the *Prayer Book for Earnest Christians*. The arrival of the new day and the gift of life this dawn represents must not be taken for granted. For if we do not experience our lives as gifts of God's grace and love, we will be unable to offer them in service to our Creator and to our neighbors. Instead, we will cling to life as our own property, to be secured and protected from all encroaching threats and demands. Beginning our prayers with an inventory of gratitude, counting our blessings, puts us in the position to accept God's answers to our prayers that we may not want to hear. Gratitude prepares us to yield in the manner of Job: "The LORD gave, and the LORD has taken away; blessed be the name of the LORD" (Job 1:21).

The second lesson was about yieldedness. Following the call of Christ in our lives is not simply a decision we make or a belief we accept. It involves yielding to habits of faith that have been passed down to us through the communion of saints—our faith ancestors as well as our faith mentors. Following this call may involve doing and saying things that may at first seem strange. However, when we subject ourselves to these habits of faith, we discover finally that these habits make us into what the God of Jesus Christ wants us to be: ambassadors of reconciliation in the new creation that is coming. Yielding to the habits of saints and mentors, prophets and apostles, prepares us to yield to God when things do not go our way, when life's disasters and tragedies hit us, when our prayers turn bitter.

The prayerful posture of gratitude and yieldedness, where we freely own our honest thoughts and feelings, prepares us daily to carry out the vocation we have for our entire lives. This is crucial because we live in a world where most people, even those who are Christians, experience calling as originating in career, not in Christ. By contrast, the Anabaptist idea of Christian calling urges us to make our membership in the body of Christ the first point of reference for all of our actions in the world, at work, at home, in church, or in the ballpark. It assumes that in the life of the church we learn habits and practices that will shape our decisions and our conduct in every aspect of our lives.

This book offers five concrete practices that we can take up expecting that through them God's grace can flow to the world in all we do. The first section leads us to discover truth in the *word* of God and in the life and discernment of the church. The second section urges us join the church and respect life given by God in the *water* of baptism. The third section invites us to give to the church and serve others by sharing bread and *wine*. In the fourth section, *we* who follow Christ encounter life in community and are encouraged to yield to the church. In the fifth and final section, we are called to be like priests who *witness* to the world in word and deed. These practices, when carried out prayerfully and in the company of believers, transform our lives into the image of Christ and make God's peace visible in our world.

Make a difference

How might all this make a difference in the world and in our own lives? The story of Juan (not his real name) illustrates one way that members of Christ's body can act together as ambassadors who make God's reconciling salvation visible in the world.

Juan has been part of my community at First Mennonite Church in Bluffton, Ohio, for the past twenty-five years. Two years ago the United States government began proceedings to deport him to Guatemala, where he was born and where he lived until 1984. Back then, he had traveled to Mexico and crossed into the United States after the Guatemalan government threatened his life because of his advocacy work on behalf of displaced peasants during the Guatemalan civil war. Although he was detained by U.S. immigration officials in 1984, he was released when First Mennonite Church paid his bail. It was part of the church's involvement in the Sanctuary Movement where American churches hosted Central American refugees on their way to Canada. Although Juan applied for asylum in the United States, it took the U.S. government twenty-two years to deny his request for asylum in 2007, in part because a deportation order against Juan had never been rescinded.

Since 2007, Juan's struggle with the U.S. Immigration and Customs Enforcement has been a nightmare for him and a reminder to our congregation that our life together is a scandal to the authorities of this world. We know that Juan is a brother in Christ and that he belongs with us. The U.S. government insists that he does not belong and that he must leave the country—although, much to our surprise, after much prayer and intercession, an appeal to reopen his deportation case was suddenly granted.

As I sat with Juan in our church fellowship hall during a fundraising meal for a youth mission project, he talked about his recent plane ride to Texas for a hearing on the reopened case. His lawyer had filed for a change of venue to a court location closer to Bluffton, Ohio, but no one had heard back about whether this request had been approved. So Juan flew to Texas, accompanied by another member of our church, where the judge asked him whether he wanted a change of venue. Juan, who had just traveled over a thousand miles to this hearing, said "yes" and the judge granted the request.

As our congregation continues to walk with Juan in his struggle to stay, jumping through one legal hoop after another, it is clear that the divided world in which we live, with its national boundaries and citizenship laws and immigration bureaucracies, is false and unreliable. In the name of our security and well-being, this false world ends up betraying what is most deeply true about human beings: we are all created in God's image and are thus brothers and sisters, not enemies or aliens. This false world not only divides us from those with whom we are meant to live in peace, it also alienates us from our very own lives and work. Sometimes, like Juan, we are exhausted by complicated and futile-seeming bureaucratic processes. At other times, we are simply unable to remember why our lives matter, why we are here.

Listening to Juan's story as we share food together, offering our time and money to support his legal case, praying for him and for his advocates as they seek justice, and worshiping the God of Israel and Jesus Christ with Juan, reminds us all of the reconciling calling of Christ which we have accepted in baptism. In response, some members of our congregation have become advocates for more just immigration laws. Others have worked to make our community a more hospitable place for immigrants, teaching Spanish to local children, for example. Some are involved in ministry in a nearby Spanish-speaking congregation. One member worked to plan an academic and church conference on the theme of immigration to raise consciousness and understanding throughout our region about the issues and obstacles faced by immigrants.

There are perhaps more subtle ways this experience has an impact on our lives and daily habits as well. Having witnessed the courage of a brother who has crossed many risky borders makes us more willing to cross borders of status, identity, and culture in our neighborhoods and workplaces. Some of us struggle to make our places of work more open to people who have often experienced discrimination and disadvantages. For all of us, our walk with Juan reminds us that the world around us is not reliable but that God's Word is.

In response to all the division and blindness around us—the sin we confront within ourselves and among us—this book offers an invitation to participate in the call to be the peaceable communal life of the people of God. In the church those who have been baptized with water and who eat the Lord's Supper are granted the opportunity to see and to embrace the world as it really is, not "from a human point of view" but from the perspective of the "new creation" that God through Jesus Christ is bringing about (2 Corinthians 5:16-17). This life together in the body of Christ involves a different vision and artful practices that free our bodies to witness to the reconciling service of Jesus Christ—the love that has overcome the world.[5] Each practice leads to new ways of seeing the world. Each is part of the church's call to join God's reconciling mission, even when we are surrounded by selfishness and violence. Finally, these practices help us remember who we are every day of our lives, whether we are beginning a new job or getting ready for retirement, whether we are starting college or starting over. We are those who belong to Jesus Christ.

For reflection and discussion

1. In what ways have you experienced dissatisfaction with your life circumstances? How do you imagine a good life?
2. When and why do you pray? What words do you use? What is the origin of the words?
3. What do you think of the Anabaptist view that life and workplace decisions by Christians should express obe-

dience to Jesus Christ? How do you make good decisions in the context of your daily work?

4. Who are the spiritual mentors in your life? What good habits have you learned from them?

5. How does our cultural climate discourage gratitude? How can the church encourage contentment and thankfulness?

WORD:
DISCOVERING TRUTH

Chapter 1

GO TO CHURCH

Every carefully considered human practice, including the Christian life, must at some point address the question of truth. On what truth can we ground our lives? And where do we find this truth?

Christians confess with John the Evangelist that Jesus Christ is "the way, and the truth, and the life" (John 14:6). If our calling as Christian disciples is life together as ambassadors of Jesus Christ, then our search for truth, for a ground of our being, must begin with the way that Jesus addressed the question of truth, with how he responded to questions about his calling.

Following the truth

When Jesus is hauled in front of Pilate to answer for his controversial actions, this Roman governor interrogates him about his mission and identity. Jesus speaks evasively at first and then makes two dramatic pronouncements: (1) the reign of God is not defended by the sword; and (2) everyone who "belongs to the truth" knows the voice of Jesus (John 18:28-38). By saying this Jesus makes it clear that practices based in the truth of God do not need to be protected or defended. Christ calls us without threatening us or forcing our assent. But this does require a response.

Pilate responds to Jesus' claims with the question that rings through the ages and that we are often tempted to echo as we hedge our own responses to the truth: "what is truth?" It is as if we are too sophisticated to be hoodwinked into naïve commitments. Like Pilate, we are able to see that what is true depends on where we stand and how we look at things. The truth of the Pharisees is not the same thing as the truth of the Sadducees. Jerusalem offers a different perspective on the world than does Rome or Athens. Realizing this can make us either cynical or curious, and it is not clear which attitude Pilate has—perhaps a mix of both.

But such hedging easily turns into one more way we seek to leverage the truth for our own purposes. Just like Pilate, we worry about how to make the truth that confronts us work out for us. We too want to control it in order to manage the outcomes. We are tempted to think this way especially when we face big decisions, like the one Pilate faces when Jesus shows up in his court.

These big decisions haunt us before and after we make them: whether and where to go to college; whether or whom to marry; which major or occupation to pursue; how to cope with conflict at work or at home or among our friends; how to spend our money or where to give it away; whether or not to have children; how to respond to the demands of our children if we have them; whether to change jobs or to stay where we are; whether to risk livelihood for principle; how to decide when the commitment to principle is an act of arrogance and when it is an expression of courage; how best to respond to the life disasters we or our friends experience; what to do in our retirement years. The list goes on.

Self-help books promise to give us handles on history, for-mulas for making our lives come out right, confidence in the face of uncertainty: *Change Your Brain, Change Your Body*; *The Belly Fat Cure*; *Life Is What You Make It*; *What to Expect When You're Expecting*. The popularity of such books is a symptom of the human desire for a manageable truth, for knowledge that puts us in the driver's seat and makes us feel, even if for a moment, as if the world was ours for the taking. This desire identifies us with Pilate's response to Jesus, a response that seeks protection from the truth or possession *of* it rather than possession *by* it—a coping strategy to deal with the appearance of the Lord of the universe in his court. Many of our responses to Jesus reflect such self-help approaches to truth. For example, we seek to reduce the way of Jesus to a manageable collection of propositions—the Four Spiritual Laws or the correct formulas of doctrine. We admire Jesus as a great teacher who embodied noble virtues and a heroic character. We turn him into our best buddy or fantasy companion. We treat Jesus as a great philosopher whose sayings can be studied for insight about the nature of things. We accept Jesus as a sacrifice that paid the debt for our sins.

These responses to Jesus, because they often reflect in part the truth of Jesus, can deflect us from encountering Jesus Christ as our Lord—the one who has accepted us and is prepared to rule our lives. They seek to possess Jesus rather than allowing him to possess us. We must come to terms with the realization that Jesus cannot be possessed or accepted, that he can only be followed as he moves through the world's history and our own. We can yield our lives to the way of Jesus Christ, but we cannot claim Jesus for our own dramas of upward mobility, status seeking, social and national security, or any of the other plots we work out to secure our lives.[1]

The truth of Jesus Christ incarnate is a social truth, not a disembodied fact. We cannot fully discover it in our minds or act on it by ourselves. We can only hear and know Jesus' voice if we become one of the sheep in his flock (John 10:27).[2] And if we are to be one of his flock, we must attend to where this flock is gathered in the world. For Christians, that place is called the church. This is not, first of all, the big building with stained glass windows in the middle of town, although we may indeed find the church there. As we will see, this defenseless church is a body on the move.

We learn from Jesus' response to Pilate that truth is not a *what* to consider, an equation to solve, or a formula to learn—useful as such things might be to get through the day. Rather, truth is a voice to which we listen, a person we are called to follow, a conviction by which we are possessed, a role that we play. Truth is a commitment to which we surrender our lives; as Christians our commitment is to the One who has already given his life for us.

No one has stated this call to truth more clearly in the modern world than Dietrich Bonhoeffer, the German Lutheran pastor and theologian who was executed for his resistance to the Nazi regime. The call of Christ, according to Bonhoeffer, is to "come and die."[3]

For Bonhoeffer, the call of Christ meant literal death; but it is also clear that in this dramatic statement, he was not speaking primarily of the death of the body. Christ calls us to the death of the self. Furthermore, this death is not the death of our ability to act; instead it liberates our actions from individualism, self-centeredness, and our need for self-protection. The death of self is the prerequisite for what Bonhoeffer calls "community with Jesus Christ," a "life together" in which we bear one another's burdens, in which we forgive one another, and in which we "know only Christ."[4] In other words, this gospel truth that possesses us makes us free, if we will but allow it, if we will but let go and give up. Thomas Merton puts it this way: "To find life, we must die to life as we know it. To find meaning, we must die to meaning as we know it."[5]

Understanding selfless freedom

After God's people Israel are liberated from slavery in Egypt, their leader, Moses, gets instructions to create a meeting place where God can be worshipped and the people reminded of who they are and to what they are called. These instructions occur while God's people are wandering in the wilderness, between the time of liberation and the entry into the Promised Land, often complaining, sometimes feeling nostalgic for the days of slavery, struggling to give up the safety and security they had experienced as slaves in Egypt.

In the midst of this loss and disorientation—of death to self and security—there is the call for God's people Israel to build a new community. It is organized around trusting and worshipping God rather than the military power of an earthly ruler. Building this obedient community requires refashioning the materials of creation into furnishings of faith where God's people can discover their true home. Precious metals, expensive gemstones, clay for sculpture, linen for the tent, and other building materials in the hands of skilled workers become the artful expression of obedience to the call of God.

For example, in Exodus 31 God calls Bezalel from the tribe of Judah and Oholiab from the tribe of Dan as leaders of the artisans who will make the beautiful furniture of the community's meeting place: the golden lampstand, the table of the bread of presence, the ark of the covenant, the altars of incense and burnt offerings, the basin, and the vestments. In the land of Egypt these leaders were slave labor, exploited for the expansion of the empire. In the context of the liberated community, however, they are devoted to expressing the divine image and intent. They are granted not only the gift of craftsmanship but also the authority of leadership and management.

Furthermore, as Waldemar Janzen points out, in this story the spiritual gifts are not "reserved . . . for the realm with which we often associate them (e.g., prayer, prophecy, etc.). Instead, they are applied to the work of artists and artisans working with tangible materials."[6]

However, says Janzen, these artists are not self-sufficient, working on their own. Rather, they are possessed by the truth of God, by the commandments of God, and by their trust in the One who brought them out of Egypt. Their artistic work contributes to the ongoing fashioning of God's people into the faithful blessing and witness to the nations—which they have always been called to be. In the same way, the call of Christ to come and die releases our God-given passions, skills, and gifts from captivity to mere pragmatism, to be offered as an expression of the divine.

In my own experience, I heard many voices urging me to suppress gifts that God has given me. During my childhood, my delight in reading was often ridiculed by peers who valued athletic activity over the mountains of books I was always reading. In college, I often felt pressure to undertake a so-called pragmatic profession, such as business administration or accounting. And, as a graduate student, my interest in teaching in the same small, church-related college where I had discovered my passions and gifts was often viewed as quaint in a world where the larger university offered the best chance of peer recognition, leisure time for research, and a good salary.

Fortunately, in all of those contexts, there were other voices urging me not to play it safe, not to be practical, and not to accept the authority of common sense. Instead, through countless conversations with faithful people, the Spirit of God nudged me to accept my own skills and interests and curiosities as gifts. Rather than fearfully ignore or repress them, I was to receive and offer them with gratitude. But the accepting of these gifts for me was an act of dying to self, not of self-advancement. If I had wanted that, I would have given attention to status and money and influence. But in giving it up I have discovered my true home.

What we like and love is the dimension of God's image reflected most in our lives. Following Jesus Christ may mean giving up our present occupations in order to discover the full truth of our places in the coming reign of God. Peter, Andrew, James, and John all left behind their fishing business and Matthew resigned from the internal revenue service. But following Christ in truth will in fact set our gifts and passions free for the cause of God. The calling of Christ is a high and holy calling that transforms our embodied desires into gifts "acceptable to God" (Romans 12:1).

The truth in the church

How do we discover the claims God's truth makes on our lives? How do we give up self for the home God has prepared for us—the "better country" for which we yearn (Hebrews 11:16)? How do we respond to Pilate's question: What is truth? The answer of the church—Christ's body in the world today—is an invitation: come and listen, come and discuss, come and see.

If we look back or glance forward from the story of Pilate's interrogation of Jesus, we find this invitation confirmed on every hand. We can rewind and find Jesus questioning the teachers in the temple (Luke 2:46) or we can fast forward and find Philip discussing the book of Isaiah with the Ethiopian eunuch (Acts 8:26-40). In practically every case where a meaningful discovery is made in the Scriptures, it is made with others. Even Paul on the road to Damascus, when he is confronted by a blinding light and a voice from heaven, is surrounded by fellow travelers at the moment of his conversion. It is also a church member, Ananias, who by laying his hands on Paul restores his sight and confirms Paul's vision and calling. Ananias tells Paul "the Lord Jesus, who appeared to you on your way here, has sent me so that you may regain your sight and be filled with the Holy Spirit" (Acts 9:17).

From this survey we conclude that *if we are to live in this Jesus-centered truth, we must go to church.* Catholics have been right all along that we cannot have a relationship with Jesus Christ without being joined to his body on earth. Protestants have been right that this body consists of all believers without distinction. And Anabaptists have been right that this believing body makes God's peace visible right now in human history. The church is indeed a flawed and broken body; yet the church is the presence of Jesus Christ in the world; "she is his new creation through water and the word," as the old hymn reminds us.[7]

Of course, going to church does not necessarily mean going to a large building on Sunday morning and sitting in a pew with members of a denomination, although on many (and even most) occasions it may mean that. Going to church is nothing more and nothing less than two or three gathered in the name of Jesus and under the guidance of the Holy Spirit, around the Word of God—the story and action of God creating and reconciling the world.

It is not enough for us as individuals to know God's story. It must be consumed and lived with brothers and sisters in Christ, so that the members of the body can thrive and grow. As young Mennonite pastor Thomas Dunn remarks, "I bother with the church for the same reason that I bother to breathe, that I bother to eat, and that I bother to drink. Just like my body would die if I did not breathe, eat, or drink, so my spiritual health would suffer and soon die without the church."[8]

I typically go to church several times a week: first on Sunday morning to a traditional worship service, including a Sunday school discussion of the Bible, second for a church committee meeting of one kind or another, third for midweek sharing of a meal and life stories, and fourth, for weekly choir practices. My congregation offers other opportunities as well: morning prayers, historical lectures, musical programs, children and youth clubs, weddings, funerals, and much more.

The way other people go to church may be very different from how I go to church. Going to church might mean more time spent informally with friends, or more music practice, or even more time alone in a study reading books. However, whether I am by myself or with others, going to church is akin to the experience of Philip and the Ethiopian eunuch: giving and receiving counsel about the meaning of the Word of God in the presence of the Holy Spirit and together answering the question of what to do with what we discover (Acts 8:34).

In my congregation we have formalized this discernment task in cases where people face a crisis or difficult decision. When one of our members faces challenging circumstances, they may ask for assistance from a discovery team consisting of members of the congregation whose gifts and life experiences are particularly suited to offer careful guidance and wise counsel.

However, the church's role in guiding our response to the call of Christ is far more than focused discussion during times of trauma. When going to church becomes a habit for us, the church's routines of worship and teaching and decision-making can become a central force in our daily routines, when we are experiencing ordinary time. Responding to the calling of Christ means that we must allow life together in the church to shape the rest of our lives.

The accounts of a tragic school shooting at Nickel Mines, Pennsylvania in 2006 highlight the mature and self-assured response of the young Amish girls who were about to be killed. After the tragedy, the Amish community also responded with forgiveness and neighborliness towards the killer's widow.

These are quite clearly not the reactions of heroic individuals who mustered extraordinary human will to go against the prevailing culture and to forgive. Rather they were knee-jerk responses of church members who had learned habits of forgiveness and yieldedness in their community life and teaching.[9] On a less dramatic but just as faithful note, a recent issue of *The Marketplace*, published by Mennonite Economic Development Associates, tells the story of Grant Unrau, owner of a successful marketing company called Stun Marketing. Unrau attributes the success of his leadership style to basic practices he learned growing up in the church and in family-owned businesses that were shaped by church values. For him, treating every employee as a partner and a complete person was not based on trendy management and motivation theories, but on deep habits gained through a life in the church. The author of the article describes Unrau's approach: "He worked as hard as everyone else and avoided lording it over others."[10]

To discuss going to church in this way may seem banal or mistaken. In North American culture many people view organized religious activities with some suspicion. They prefer pursuing some kind of individual, personal experience with God. Polls show clearly that many more North Americans claim to believe in God than actually attend church regularly.[11]

I recently talked with a college graduate who grew up in the church but who confessed he hasn't had much time for church in recent years. "I've needed to take some time off from church," he said. "I'm still a spiritual person, it's just organized religion that I'm taking a break from." This might be a helpful reminder for some believers that a given practice of organized faith cannot by itself contain the work and will of God.

At the same time, a posture of spiritual independence cannot be sustained in the long haul. Christianity that represents Jesus Christ and the reconciling work of God cannot exist except as a faith that is organized in some way. Without the company of believers to surround and sustain us, our discipleship simply falls apart. Anabaptists like Pilgram Marpeck contend that through baptism a believer "enters into the body of Christ, that is, the church of Christ, yes, into Christ Himself, as the true ark wherein, through the word of obedience, one can be preserved from the flood."[12] Without the church, the truth delivered by Jesus is obscured, and thus we are also ultimately lost.[13]

The centrality of the church may seem like a preposterous claim. In our time, a church community is seen as provincial, having a narrow and prejudiced view of the world. Pursuing the truth can free us from that kind of church. While the historical church is a flawed and frustrating failure much of the time, it is nevertheless the vehicle by which God has chosen to continue the saving work of Jesus Christ.

The book *Hiking Through* by Paul V. Stutzman illustrates this discovery of both the failure and hope of the church. The book describes his struggle to find God following the untimely death of his wife and his experience of deep, inescapable grief. In the midst of loss and disorientation, Stutzman remembered his dream to hike the Appalachian Trail—the full 2,176 miles from Georgia to Maine. He decided to fulfill this dream; he quit his well-paying job of twenty-five years as the manager of a successful restaurant and exchanged the comforts and familiarity of home for the uncertain wilderness of the Trail.

Although he writes affectionately of the Amish-Mennonite community that nurtured him from birth and acquainted him with the God of the Bible, he also recognizes that the rules and boundaries of that community were obstacles to an adventurous and thriving relationship with the living God. A motley group of Appalachian Trail characters with whom he hiked and conversed became friends and helped him encounter the presence of God amidst the challenges of the hike. As someone who spent a good deal of his life being in charge, Stutzman came to depend on the generosity and hospitality of others. Other people provided what Stutzman calls "trail magic"—unexpected gifts of food and drink to hikers, motorists who offered rides into a nearby town for food and lodging or traveling companions who shared advice, supplies and theological insight.[14]

By accepting the rupture of the well-established and entirely valid routines that had shaped and secured his life, Stutzman was able both to recognize the goodness of these routines and to acknowledge their inadequacy to a life of faith. Living for a few months with the vulnerability of life on the trail, depending only on the supplies he could carry on his back and on the generosity of others, he was able to encounter the God of Jesus Christ in a way that had eluded him before. But this encounter was social. It involved the congregation of Appalachian Trail travelers, each with their own wounds and gifts to contribute to his renewed discovery of God. Through these new friends, and amidst the wonders of creation, Stutzman was able to go back to church in a way that reinvigorated his calling as a disciple of Jesus Christ. [15]

Going to church is not a call to be a passive consumer of familiar routines in our own comfortable corner of the world that neglect the love of God for the whole creation. Going to church is rather a call for engagement of active Spirit-guided participation in the struggle to make God's peaceable reign visible—even when the church as an institution might forget the Lord it represents. Going to church means asking together with other brothers and sisters what it means to be faithful to the God who has been revealed in Jesus Christ and in the Scriptures. When we turn to that revelation of God in Jesus Christ, we discover that the church as Christ's body is a community that exceeds the boundaries of nation, tribe, or race. The church, when it is faithful, manifests the work of God in Christ reconciling all things and becoming a blessing to the nations. Thus, the church, to be faithful to its calling, must continually remind itself of that call and ask again what it means in our time and place. It does this by returning to the Scriptures from which it receives its mandate and discovers its own story—the story of Abraham and Sarah, Moses and Miriam, Samuel and Saul, Ruth and Naomi, Jeremiah and Jesus and Paul and Lydia—the story of Israel and the church. (For a helpful review and summary of this ancient story, see the website for *Go to Church* at: www.MennoMedia.org/GotoChurch.) In the next chapter I discuss how to relate this biblical story to our lives today.

For reflection and discussion

1. What sources (authors, websites, periodicals, people) do you trust for the truth? How do you know that these sources are trustworthy?

2. How do you go about making the big decisions of your life? Who do you involve in the decision? Who do you exclude? Why?

3. What activities and interests give the most meaning to your life? What are the experiences and involvements you are most passionate about? What role should this orientation to the world play in your life decisions?

4. If you go to church, why do you go to church? If not, why not?

5. Do you agree with the claim that the church is necessary to sustain the Christian life? Why or why not? Can you think of instances where going to church poses an obstacle to Christian faith?

Chapter 2

READ THE BIBLE

It is not enough to go to church. We must also read the Bible, the book of the church, so that we know what we are supposed to do. Karl Barth puts this point very succinctly, "We will not be obedient to the Church but to the Word of God, and therefore in the true sense to the Church."[1] Or as an Anabaptist hymn claims more poetically: "The Word of God is solid ground."[2]

To say that Christian discovery begins with the Word of God as found in Scriptures is not to say that the only place we discover the truth of God is in the Bible, as we will see later on. It means that reading and discussing the Bible together with other believers shapes the way we view the world around us.

Sometimes those who rightly lift up the Bible as God's inspired Word also wrongly assume that the Bible contains a simple message—and that our primary response should be to accept or reject it. But the Bible itself makes it clear that receiving God's Word through the Scriptures is not merely a matter of assent to simple truth claims or a checklist of correct conclusions. While there is surely an intellectual dimension to Bible reading, John of Patmos was called to eat the scroll of Scripture. This suggests that the Bible introduces us to a meal that we mull over and chew on, receiving spiritual nutrition that invades and pervades our lives. When John does eat the scroll, it involves the bodily experiences of both sweetness and bitterness, of both delight and sorrow (Revelation 10:10).

At least three practices are critical to a full experience of biblical discovery. They can help us read the Bible well and also discover truth in our daily lives when we need to make decisions. The practices I want to discuss here include discerning the text, applying the text, and performing the text.

For these practices to work well, it is best to have a general knowledge of the larger biblical story from Genesis to Revelation and to be part of a group that discusses the Bible together. If you are new to the Bible, there are a number of summaries and abridged versions available to get you started—including my own, available at this book's website (www.MennoMedia. org/GotoChurch). Of course, in the long run, the best way to know the Bible is to read through it in a readable, contemporary translation—possibly using a Bible reading plan.[3]

Discerning the text

My own encounter with the Bible happens most vividly and powerfully in a weekly Sunday school class I attend—the Sojourners class at First Mennonite Church in Bluffton, Ohio. I will draw on experiences in this class to describe these Bible reading practices.

We often begin our class by expressing our honest questions and reactions to the text in front of us including frustration, doubt, anger, trauma, wonder, delight, and inspiration. Why does God destroy the earth with a flood? Why does Israel keep forgetting to follow God's ways? Why does Leviticus forbid wearing clothes made of both wool and linen? What is the relationship between God's righteousness and God's love? Why does Paul seem so arrogant at times? Was John hallucinating on Patmos?

In our class, we take turns leading discussions; each person typically has a different approach to shaping our discernment about the text's setting and probable meaning. Some of us lead by summarizing Bible commentaries; others explore the psychological or political meanings of the text; still others take a more devotional approach, emphasizing the apparent spiritual or experiential dimensions.

More often than not, we end up reading passages coming before and after the selected text to strengthen our understanding of the broader narrative context. And we take turns reading the Scripture text itself, each of us lending our distinct voice and inflection to the words on the page—words that we now hear as a gathered body. Sometimes we sing hymns that deepen or complicate the apparent themes of the reading.

We typically draw our conclusions about the meaning of the text with an eye to the rest of the Bible, keeping in mind that there may be contrasting conclusions from other passages. In fact, we assume that an honest investigation of the Bible "contains multitudes"—to use a phrase by Walt Whitman—or, as Walter Brueggemann says of the Old Testament, this text is the site of "ongoing, unsettled dispute."[4]

Early Anabaptist Bible readers insisted that this recognition of the complex and even contradictory quality of the text be made part of the process of interpretation. Writers like Hans Denck published lists of contradictory biblical statements to call attention to this aspect of the Bible.[5] Balthasar Hubmaier warned that refusing to recognize contradictory aspects of the Bible leads to believing "half-truth" and results in "sects, quarrels, and heresies." For Hubmaier, those who proof-text—defending doctrinal or ethical positions on the basis of only one scriptural statement—are "doing patchwork with the Scripture, not comparing opposing Scripture and uniting both into a whole judgment."[6]

One way our Sunday school class copes with the Bible's contrasting convictions and claims is to remember the unfolding story or drama within which these claims are made. We remind ourselves again and again that the Bible is a record of God's grand and unfolding project to renew and reconcile the world so lovingly created and for which God died through Jesus Christ.

As followers of Jesus Christ, Anabaptists saw his life, teachings, death, and resurrection as decisive interventions into the conflicted world of the Bible. They were convinced by the arguments that Jesus makes in the Gospels while engaging with the Hebrew Bible. Our class also largely accepts this

Anabaptist alignment with Jesus Christ as the first and final authority of biblical discernment. We often ask the question: "how would Jesus respond to this issue; how would Jesus read this text?"

This way of reading the Bible accepts the authority of Jesus and considers the arguments in the biblical story which seem to challenge our perspective of Jesus. This follows the non-oppositional approach that Jesus modeled: "You have heard that it was said, 'An eye for an eye and a tooth for a tooth.' But I say to you, Do not resist an evildoer" (Matthew 5:38-39). Here Jesus both acknowledges and challenges a conventional scriptural conclusion but preserves the perspective that he is opposing.

Such a way of practicing Bible reading serves us well in a conflicted and pluralistic world. The world of the Bible is not a narrow, predictable world that only confirms what we already think we know. It is a conflicted world that challenges us at every turn, especially when we place our trust for the journey of discovery into the hands of Jesus Christ—the Word made flesh.

The conflicts that emerge in our discussions, especially when they deal with controversial issues such as sexuality or politics, are not seen as problems to be solved so much as occasions for spiritual discovery and regeneration. The conflicted world of the Spirit-inspired Scriptures enables us to see our own conflicts as signs of the Holy Spirit's presence. We know that when the wind of the Spirit blows, there will be both conflict and peace, as in the biblical story itself. We also know that the unity of the Spirit of which we are assured is not something we can manufacture; it is a gift to be received, often when we have failed to achieve unity on our own terms.

Applying the text

Next, our class typically seeks to make some kind of application to our own lives. We recognize that we are making a great leap from a strange and ancient text into our present familiar world. On the other hand, when we have immersed ourselves in the Bible, our present world may appear strange from the perspective of the Scriptures. For example, the complex tribal dramas of Old Testament patriarchal history can make the nuclear family of our present world seem shallow and incomplete—even if more free and fair. Or, the detailed legal codes of Leviticus can challenge our focus on faith as a set of abstract beliefs rather than as obedient practices.

When believers gather in study and worship, the presence and power of the Holy Spirit fills this gap between the Bible and our lives. So we ask: "What does it mean in our time and place to follow Jesus' call to proclaim liberty to captives and sight to the blind, to turn the other cheek, to go the extra mile, to proclaim good news—to accept the great commission as ours (Luke 4; Matthew 28:16-20)? We may not necessarily agree on the answer; but we learn to see our mission and calling in new ways.

One reason for taking up difficult questions in church settings is the diversity of gifts within the body as we reflect about how to apply biblical wisdom. When we consider what it means to walk an extra mile carrying an enemy's bags, it might be helpful to have someone present who has lived under occupation; when we discuss what it means to proclaim liberty to captives, someone who has been to prison; when we talk about what it means to redistribute our wealth according to the debt-forgiveness principles of Jubilee, someone who has experienced poverty; and when we consider what it means to live by the inclusiveness of the great commission to incorporate all nations in the new humanity, someone who has experienced discrimination.

In our Sojourners class, we have college students and retirees; people born in the United States, in Canada, and in El Salvador; women and men; singles and married people. The diversity of backgrounds and perspectives helps us think about how the biblical text might be speaking to us in ways that challenge our habits and assumptions. Because all are unlikely to see the same implications, we must subject our own views and lives to the Spirit-inspired words that emerge when the body of Christ gathers around the Word.[7]

Seeking the implications of the biblical world for our own world and for our lives is important because the church is a community that has been founded on Jesus Christ, the incarnate Word, God made flesh (1 Corinthians 3:11). When the Word became flesh and dwelt among us, this posed a profound challenge to the Greek philosophical view of truth as an abstraction or an ideal in our minds that floats beyond the grasp of our mortal bodies. When we seek the truth of God by placing ourselves under the rule of Christ, we cannot keep truth at arm's length nor control it for our own purposes. Our lives must necessarily be transformed by that truth. In fact, Anabaptists went so far as to insist that the only way to understand the truth of the Bible was to begin acting according to it.

Arnold Snyder has put this point very succinctly: "For the Anabaptists, learning, remembering, and repeating the words of Scripture was a means to a practical end: it was living the Bible continually that really counted."[8] Or we can recall the famous words of Hans Denck: "No one can know Christ without following him in life."[9]

Performing the text

Our Sunday school class moves again and again from a discussion of the text to an enactment of the text. Once a month we have a class potluck, in which we share food and conversation together around the table. We extend our own financial resources to others through *white gift* offerings contributed to church and community organizations at the conclusion of Advent. We assist one another with tasks such as child care and transportation and bear one another's burdens through prayer and encouragement.

Sometimes this Anabaptist emphasis on deeds in response to words is seen as a formula where practical outcomes take precedence over contemplative or intellectual inquiries. This is a mistake, in my view. The point is to allow the communal engagement with the Bible to shape our lives. Sara Wenger Shenk, in a book entitled *Anabaptist Ways of Knowing* emphasizes how knowledge in the Anabaptist tradition has often been experienced through body and habit more than through beliefs and ideas.[10] Participating in service projects, or wearing plain and simple clothing, or practicing enemy love, are ways to know Jesus Christ.

Reading the Bible together with our brothers and sisters is an intellectual, bodily, and spiritual experience that shapes our responses to other discussions and contexts of inquiry, including those of family life and the workplace. It is an intellectual experience insofar as Bible study involves examining a text, seeking some kind of coherence or meaning, and discussing the emerging ideas and convictions with others. It is a bodily experience insofar as the discussions often arouse feelings of enthusiasm, anger, excitement, sadness, and frustration; and insofar as our senses are engaged with the sounds, sights, smells, touch, and tastes of a gathering of people scrunched in a circle talking, listening, drinking coffee, and awaiting the Holy Spirit. Finally, reading the Bible together carries with it a spiritual dimension of expecting the unexpected, seeking the lost, recognizing what had been missing, and discovering what had not yet been seen. This is the experience the disciples had on the road to Emmaus (Luke 24:13-35) and when they were gathered together on the day of Pentecost (Acts 2). They found that when they were together as a body, in conversation, and open to the Spirit, they were able to see what they had not seen before: the glorified Christ, the neighbor's gift, the world reconciled.

For reflection and discussion

1. How challenging is it for you to understand the Bible? How has your understanding of the Bible changed over time? Do you agree that the Bible is best understood in the company of other believers? Why or why not?
2. If you attend a Sunday school class, how does your class differ from the class described in this chapter? Are there important ways of discovering truth that are missing from the account of the Sojourners class?
3. Try to remember some times when you followed a biblical commandment or principle and came to

understand the commandment differently as a result
of following it.
4. What unique life experiences have helped you understand or appreciate specific parts of the Bible?
5. Name the parts of the Bible that perplex you or that you
dislike. As believers, how should we respond to Bible
passages that we experience as confusing or offensive?

NOTE: You may want to read an overview of the biblical
story to recall primary biblical themes. Your group may also
wish to devote a separate session to this review. The summary included at this book's website (www.MennoMedia.org/
GotoChurch) includes study questions for such an exercise.

Chapter 3

SEE THE WORLD

For Christians, the created world around us is part of the book we read for signs of God's truth. However, our life together with other Bible-reading believers makes it possible for us to see more clearly the truth of God in the delightful and awe-inspiring world around us.

Christians in the Reformed tradition such as the Presbyterians are fond of saying that "All truth is God's truth," an adage which implies that truth can be found anywhere, not simply in the church or in the Bible. In the Anabaptist tradition this saying could more helpfully be rendered: all truth is *Christ's* truth. In Jesus Christ, the firstborn of creation, we have discovered a way of thinking, living, and dying that works—in the words of John Howard Yoder—"with the grain of the universe."[1] Wherever we find the reconciling work of Jesus Christ manifested we will recognize it, study it, affirm it, and stand with it. Two crucial biblical principles prepare us to see the world around us in its God-created loveliness: (1) the suffering of creatures as a source of renewed life; and (2) the humility of blindness as a condition for expanded sight. These two principles can help us avoid allowing the demands of our occupations to replace our calling to the life and body of Christ.

Suffering and creation

Anabaptists like Pilgram Marpeck and Hans Hut described a gospel of the creatures that revealed the truth of Christ to the world when the Scriptures themselves were neglected or misinterpreted. Marpeck wrote, "All visible creatures are placed in the world as apostles and teachers."[2]

One of the lessons taught by the creatures about the Word is the role of suffering and death in re-creation and renewal. The circle of life that we observe around us involves the energetic living and eventual consumption of plants and animals that serve one another as nutrients and protein. Just as plants and animals live on in the human beings and other animals that consume them, so must we "die to the world in order to live in God," as Hans Hut put it.[3]

Our view of this sacrificial circle of life is shaped by the stories in the Bible where new life flows from sacrifice and resurrection supersedes death. Serving others, even unto death, is the way to new life. Death does not need to be feared for it does not have the last word, either in the Bible or in the created world around us. Those who give their lives will gain them, according to the gospel. And Jesus Christ, who gave up equality with God to become a suffering human being, now rules the cosmos because of his defining act of loving and sacrificial service (Philippians 2:1-11).

This perspective challenges standard understandings of science, history, sociology, economics, and even agriculture, which say the world is created and sustained through domination and violence. Instead, through the lens of the salvation story in the Bible, we see that the universe is ruled by those who serve it and who offer their lives to others. The gospel of the creatures confirms and illuminates the gospel of the Prince of Peace, Jesus Christ.[4]

Operating from such a perspective, a cell biologist might propose nonviolent metaphors to describe cell behavior that is usually accounted for with violent images or stories in which some cells are "killer cells" fighting against "invading viruses," for example. A historian might retell history from the standpoint of neglected actions of nonviolent social movements rather than from the standpoint of the presumed ultimate power of military and coercive state action. A business educator might offer organizational management models that include concern for human dignity and well-being as more significant goals than profit and growth.[5] A farmer might decide to employ organic or natural methods of crop and livestock production rather than using chemicals that do violence to God's creation. Families and even congregations might decide to reduce the use of technologies such as automobiles and electronic communication devices that undermine the peace of their communities and of the planet, following the example of the Amish. Some families in my church have decided to live without television, for example. In my family, we have decided to take a sabbatical from electronic communication technology—including television, cell phones, and the Internet—at least one day each week, usually on Sunday.

Perhaps most importantly, not resisting the suffering that is part of the human condition strengthens our capacity for empathy and solidarity with all those who suffer in this world. The experience of suffering is something we can share in common with anyone, rich or poor. Solidarity with those who suffer is a powerful and redemptive way to see the world around us.

Humility and sight

Just as the gospel of the creatures confirms that suffering is a source of life and hope, the experience of blindness confirms that humility enables larger vision. Jesus teaches that recognizing our own blindness is what makes faithful sight possible (John 9:39-41). Confirming this view, philosopher Jacques Derrida comments, "the word that is sent, the word of *judgment* or *salvation*, the good news, always *happens* or *comes to blindness*."[6]

In his discussion of biblical figures who suffer blindness—Isaac, Eli, Tobit[7]—Derrida notes that blindness is associated with losses or sacrifices that prepare the way for an encounter with a truth beyond the apparent or visible world. Isaac mistakenly passes on the blessing to the son he does not prefer (Genesis 27), Eli's disobedient sons are killed and the ark of the covenant captured by Israel's enemies (1 Samuel 3–4), and Tobit's son departs for a journey from which his father fears he will not return (Tobit 11). In each case, a sacrifice precedes faithful knowledge—that is, knowledge without sight. And the form this knowledge takes is blessing and gratitude. Isaac blesses without knowing who he is blessing; Eli accepts the Lord's judgment against his household before his fall to death on the day of disaster; and Tobit blesses God's name when his son applies fish gall to his eyes and restores his sight. These stories witness to the capacity in faith to recognize the gift of truth that is not available to the eye or to ordinary sight, or to careful observation.

We also know from living in this world that some of our greatest discoveries about the meaning and purpose of life occur at moments of confusion and uncertainty. For example, college students often report that their most intense learning occurred during experiences where they encountered a culture or a community whose habits completely disoriented them at first.

Consider the blindness Saul of Tarsus experiences when he first hears the call of Christ on the road to Damascus (Acts 9:3-9). Saul was an enemy of the church when he was blinded on the road to Damascus in his life-changing encounter with Jesus Christ. "Why do you persecute me?" Jesus asked him. In response to this devastating question, Saul fell down, unable to see or eat or drink (Acts 9:4). Saul's encounter with Jesus Christ shattered the order of his world; instead of focusing on the threat posed by his enemies, he now was confronted by his own persecuting activity, by the enemy that he himself was.

This story of Saul's call illustrates the role that blindness and confusion play in Christ's call; blindness and call are two sides of the same coin. When Saul responds to this blinding call in obedience, he finds himself in the company of people he considered his enemies. Ananias calls him "brother Saul" and lays his hands on him to restore his sight. Saul is baptized and after taking some food, regains his strength (Acts 9:17-18).

We too are called to encounter the living God in the shape of Christ's body in the world. When we accept this call to give up what we know and what we can see for the truth that sets us free, we, like Saul, will regain our sight and our strength. Only now, we see the world no longer from a human point of view, but from the standpoint of a new creation and the ministry of reconciliation Christ has given us (2 Corinthians 5:16-19).

My friend Scott Schomburg experienced this blinding transformation when he visited an African family who had been infected with the AIDS virus. He describes his own fear as he approached the family's hut, a fear magnified by the apparent horror of the villagers at his willingness to enter a space marked by disease and death. The fear that Scott felt is the kind of fear that all of us feel when we encounter unfamiliar forms of suffering, suffering we would rather not see and from which we typically avert our gaze. Yet, when Scott crossed that threshold of fear and found himself in relationship with the members of the afflicted family he discovered joy and hope and a new perspective—witnessed most visibly by a child in the family who radiated the light of Jesus Christ in eagerly hugging Scott. This experience changed not only his perspective on the world but also his actions in the world. He now sees his own vocation from the standpoint of those who suffer, the world of peace and justice that is coming into the present blinded and broken world, the world and reign of God.[8]

The practices of going to church and reading the Bible help us see the whole world, including those parts of it that are neglected by common sense and the habits of individualism, efficiency, and self-protection. In church, we are called to see and minister to the suffering that surrounds us, to discover amidst that suffering the presence of God, who suffers with us, and who also suffers for us. This capacity to see what is otherwise invisible is a gift that is received along with the call to follow Jesus Christ.

Thus, the most important decision for a person who seeks to follow Christ is not which occupation to choose but whether to accept the gifts of suffering and blindness that are part of the call to be the church. In our society, as throughout much of human history, our preoccupation with the goods associated with paid occupations poses an obstacle to heavenly sight—blinded and suffering sight. But Jesus assures us that when we stop striving to secure our own lives—food, clothing, shelter, salaries—in order to serve God's upside-down kingdom, our lives will in fact be saved, our sight will be restored, and we will have what we need to be human, that is, to be God's children. We will see the birds of the air and the lilies of the field and know that we are loved (Matthew 6:25-33).

Stations and occupations

If God calls us to see the world around us from the reconciling perspective of Jesus Christ, and therefore from the perspective of those who suffer, then our Christian calling must be distinguished from the time-consuming and often dehumanizing demands made on us by our jobs. Quentin Schultze, a communication professor at Calvin College, has written an account of Christian calling from a Reformed theological perspective. He makes clear the difference between the vocation shared by all believers—the call to follow Jesus Christ—and the stations in which we find ourselves, the roles we take up in our "jobs, situations, and relationships."[9] This is a useful way of thinking about the relationship between the obligations we respond to at any given moment and the overarching call to give ourselves to Christ which should shape the way we conduct ourselves. Whether we are students, workers, managers, parents, caregivers, retirees, siblings, volunteers, or administrators, our Christian calling is to serve God by serving our neighbors, to participate in the reconciling work of Jesus Christ in our daily life. When we give ourselves first to Christ, we discover many opportunities to share the peace and love of Christ in the context of our stations, and to shape the relationships within those stations according to the self-sacrificial and neighbor-serving way of Jesus Christ.

However, we may also find that our present stations undermine our freedom to respond to the call of Jesus Christ. We may find ourselves in a station, such as a military career, that demands we take the life of a fellow human being or produce a product, such as tobacco or pornography, that harms others. In this case we must follow the rule established by the apostle Peter to serve God rather than human authority (Acts 5:29).

Since the United States attacked Iraq in 2003, hundreds of conscientious objectors have sought a discharge from the armed forces because they realized that they could not take the life of another human being. One objector writes of his experience in Iraq: "I was disgusted by my own reflection in the mirror. I saw and did things there that should never be viewed as acceptable by civilized people. I have been shot at, I have been mortared, I have destroyed the livelihood of innocent people, and I have seen men rejoice in the torment of others."[10] Another explains how he came to see that participating in war contradicted the teachings of Jesus: "In my Bible I continually and consistently read about how peaceful Jesus was and how many times he preached that we should love one another. Through this, I deepened my realization that I was not able to consciously carry out war, or its preparations, because I believe that it harms the spreading of the gospel and ignores the nonviolent teachings of Jesus."[11]

The discovery that as believers who have responded to the call of Christ we cannot participate in practices that harm or degrade our fellow human beings applies to more than the enterprise of war. If we need to make or sell products that do more harm than good, such as cigarettes or pornography or deadly weapons, we will need to leave our occupational home and seek a better station.

We may also find that our job undermines our own humanity, an experience that exploited workers share around the globe and throughout human history. In some work contexts, this can mean that our particular strengths and gifts are overlooked by a management system that prefers predictability and stereotypes to innovation. In other contexts, we may find that our work is evaluated according to our willingness to put our jobs ahead of our family life. Whether our job requires us to exploit others or whether we find our own humanity undermined by our work, the liberating call of Christ is the same call heard by the people of Israel and by Pharaoh's regime: "Let my people go." This is a call to holiness, to sanctification by the Lord who releases us from the slavery of Egypt (Leviticus 22:31-33). Just as God's people were called to separate themselves from the imperial culture that enslaved them, so we are called to be set apart from the social and economic structures that seek to name us and enslave us, whether that be a modern state, a corporation, or a profession. To be sanctified is to have God bring us out of whatever Egypt is enslaving.

This call to holiness was transmitted by Moses, rejected by Pharaoh, and accepted by Israel. Both Israel and Pharaoh were enslaved by the powers of empire; both were tempted to accept the security of violence and exploitation over the freedom of justice and reconciliation. Israel, even after being liberated, was tempted with nostalgia for the days of slavery and certainty. But God's call comes to kings and slaves alike: let go and give it up.

When we accept that call to holiness and lay down our lives, we are led to the waters of baptism. Just as Israel experienced the waters washing away the imperial powers of enslavement at the banks of the Red Sea, so we can experience the overpowering and cleansing waters of baptism sweeping away all that prevents us from serving God with heart, soul, and mind.

The Word of God calls us to baptism, not because the water saves us, but because in baptism we act out our submission to the creative and transforming power of God—that power that called the very world into existence using words.

Likewise, using words reminds us that our lives are a gift rooted in the creativity of God's Word and therefore can be re-created by that Word. By the power of the Word of God the water was separated from the land, and by the power of that Word we are separated by the water of baptism from all the worldliness that makes for death and from all that compromises holiness.

The Word of God exceeds the words we use, however. When we speak of God, we are reminded that God's Word is not our word, and we "recognize both that we should speak of God and yet cannot, and by that very recognition give God the glory."[12] This well-known quote from Karl Barth captures eloquently God's call to blindness—a call to see and address what we cannot fathom. Such blindness transforms our relationship to the world around us by aligning us with the suffering love of Jesus Christ and by reconciling us to the whole creation.

For reflection and discussion

1. How does the natural world reveal the knowledge of God to you? Which is more significant for understanding God: creation or the Bible?

2. Describe experiences in which blindness and confusion came before greater understanding or in which suffering prepared the way for new life.

3. Have you ever been asked to do something that you believed was wrong in the setting of a job? How did you respond? Would you act differently in the future?

4. List all the stations of life in which you are involved. What are some opportunities that you have in each of these stations to be an ambassador for Jesus Christ?

5. Have you ever felt exploited in a work context or life station? How did you respond? What are some ways to live in the freedom of Jesus Christ, while living in a world that dehumanizes us?

WATER:
RESPECTING LIFE

Chapter 4

JOIN THE CHURCH

Yielding to the call of Christ leads us to the water of baptism. When we submit to the water, we testify to the new sight we have received and we acknowledge with gratitude and reverence the life of the whole creation. This new sight—of the real, reconciled, beautiful life that God is re-creating from the ruins of the world—is our life together as ambassadors for Christ. The story of Saul's conversion and transformation into the apostle Paul shows us how the dawning of this new reality leads to water baptism, attachment to the church, and love for the whole tender and terrifying creation.

The church as enemy

We may or may not have the dramatic conversion experience Saul had. However, the call that came to Paul comes to all of us who discover our own blindness and seek to be joined with the community of new sight founded by Jesus Christ. In Saul's experience, answering the call of Christ essentially meant going to church, being baptized, and being reconciled to his "enemies." That same call reaches us today through the ongoing visible presence of the church in the world.

The reality is that for many of us, that church is a disappointing presence in the world. The call to join the church may seem like a call to become part of something dreary or wearisome or even upsetting. In many cases, the church's members act in ways that are embarrassing or that seem unfaithful to the gospel of Jesus Christ. The church probably includes people whose views and habits we might find offensive or even silly. Yet, like Saul, we are called to join the church and in this way to be joined to our enemies.

In Saul's case, Ananias is the ambassador whom God calls to go meet, greet, and baptize him. Ananias is already baptized, but he still needs to be reminded of the meaning of his baptism. He is reluctant to embrace a perceived enemy of the church: "Lord, I have heard from many about this man, how much evil he has done to your saints in Jerusalem." But the Lord says, "Go" (Acts 9:10-19).

When Ananias touches Saul and calls him a brother, "something like scales" falls from Saul's eyes. After that, Saul gets up and is baptized.

Being touched and being called; these experiences come before being reconciled and being sent. Like Saul, when in our search for truth we discover our own blindness; when we realize that our self-confident and self-righteous crusades against our "enemies" are nothing but "filthy rags," (Isaiah 64:6 NIV)—we are then called by Jesus Christ to listen to those who name us as brothers and sisters. We are called, in other words, to be touched by, and to be joined to, the body of Christ in order to receive our sight along with the Holy Spirit. Strangers are now family and enemies are friends, through the work of Jesus Christ and the power of the Holy Spirit.

The church as friendship

The story of David Morrow's reconciliation with an enemy is an amazing witness to the transformation of enemies into friends that is associated with baptism and church-joining. Morrow and his wife, Irene, were Mennonite Central Committee service workers in El Salvador during the civil war of the 1980s. They were constantly harassed by the El Salvadoran army that camped out in their backyard and that suspected the Morrows of assisting the guerrillas who were trying to overthrow the government. For the Morrows, the

El Salvadoran army became an enemy toward whom they felt bitterness and anger, even though they were pacifists.

After the Morrows returned to the United States in 1990 they began working with refugees from Latin America in Harlingen, Texas. One day, during a church service at a nearby congregation, a Salvadoran man who recognized them from their time in El Salvador greeted them. He told them that he was one of the soldiers camped out in their back yard who had made their lives so difficult. His name was Doroteo Rivera; he was seeking asylum in the United States and asked the Morrows for help with translation at his hearing. Eventually, he told them his story of joining the El Salvadoran army, becoming a member of an elite special forces battalion trained by the United States military, and being assigned to spy on their family. After being wounded, he deserted the army and escaped to the United States where he was invited to attend the Mennonite church in Brownsville, Texas. There—along with the empowerment to end his abuse of alcohol and drugs—he discovered new hope in Christ and a call to the ministry. He also discovered his former enemies, the Morrows, and they eventually became close friends. In being joined to the church of Jesus Christ, the Morrows and Doroteo Rivera discovered that enemies have indeed become friends through the power of Jesus' resurrection and the movement of the Holy Spirit.[1]

This story offers a powerful witness to God's peaceable reign. For those who read about it in the church press, it presents an alternative perspective on the world to what is found in standard media outlets—which tend to stress the ever-present violence and death as the normal state of affairs. This dramatic story also signals how being joined to the church of Jesus Christ brings us into the reconciling dawn of God's great salvation.

We do not need to travel to a war zone to experience division, alienation, and the appearance of so-called enemies. Contemporary organizational life divides us from one another according to job titles, managerial flow charts, salary bases, and departmental roles. Political systems color us red or blue and oppose us to the conservatives or the liberals. Families experience sibling rivalry and the bitterness of divorce. Even in the church, doctrinal differences and move-ment labels—evangelical, mainline, megachurch, emergent, missional, and denominational—create competing and some-times destructive factions.

Yet joining the church, even a conflicted church, offers a perspective for the long haul. It helps us remember that we are being sent as lights of love to shine amid the dark divi-sions of the world. Joined to the church we remember that in Jesus Christ, from the perspective of eternity, the dividing walls have been broken down and our enemies have been rec-onciled to us. We can now face the whole of God's good cre-ation, even our enemies, with reverence and respect.

For reflection and discussion

1. If you are a church member, what difference has it made in your life? If not, what difference do you expect it might make?

2. What are some things about the world that frighten you? How does your perspective change as someone who has been joined to the church?

3. How should a church that takes baptism seriously respond to conflicts among its members?

4. Think of people who you have considered to be your enemies. How does being joined to the church in bap-tism change your relationship to these enemies?

5. What motivated Saul to join the church, even though it meant completely renouncing his former life and name? What motivates you to join the church or to remain joined to it?

Chapter 5

BE BAPTIZED

While being joined to the church empowers us to live together with other believers in the renewed reality, the blinded world remains deluded in its division and violence. And because that worldly blindness is contagious, nothing less than the washing of baptism will save our sight. Baptism recalls for us that we are wonderful creations of God. It helps us see that our bodies are holy—temples of the Holy Spirit—and that God has created the bodies of our enemies with the same love and care that God created us.

Writing in the mid-eighteenth century, Henry Funk asserts that when believers are buried with Christ in baptism they become, body and soul, members of Christ. They are prepared to bear the cross, even at the cost of earthly goods or of life and blood. They are willing to "die the death of a martyr, and be buried," in order to "rise with Christ in glory."[1] During baptism, this experience of first being buried and then rising to new life is performed by bowing beneath or plunging into the water and then rising to be greeted and accepted into the renewed life of Christ's body.

When we publicly submit to the flowing water—whether we are immersed, doused, or sprinkled—we accept the overwhelming and cleansing grace of God found in creation—be it human, animal, plant, dirt, water, or fire. This cleansing and reconciling grace is the true *grain of the universe* to which we give ourselves in baptism and cross-bearing.

Menno Simons writes that in baptism, Christian believers "become followers of Abraham" when they "bury the old life of sin and arise with Christ to newness of life." He stresses that this Christian inheritance is "not to possess a literal kingdom and land and to become a great people," but rather "for the sake of the Word and its witness to bear all manner of anxiety, distress, and misery upon the earth; to turn the heart away from all visible and perishable things; to die unto pomp, pride, the world, flesh and blood, and thus to walk in our weakness as Christ has walked in his perfection."[2]

When we walk in our weakness we become part of what theologian Thomas F. Reynolds calls a "vulnerable communion" where disability becomes a gift instead of a defect.[3] This community not only transcends nation and culture but also changes our very understanding of humanity. Rather than judging others and ourselves according to models of perfection, we see that our brokenness and limits are what make us truly human. In this brokenness that we share with all humanity, God is present with us and embraces us through Jesus Christ.[4] In other words, in baptism we come to see our weakness and that of our neighbors as blessings rather than as defects. Weakness binds us together with Jesus Christ and with our brothers and sisters.

Christian employers—who are attached to this body of weakness—are able to recognize the gifts that people with disabilities offer as potential employees. Families who are rooted in this vulnerable communion will welcome into their midst children with developmental disabilities like Down syndrome or autism. Educators will ensure that the perspective of weakness brought by disabled students is fully acknowledged and heard in the classroom. Indeed, all who are attached to Christ's body will now seek to prepare a place of honor in their communities for the "least of these" (Matthew 25:40), including facilities that are accessible and practices that are welcoming.

Baptism and memory

The bodily action of church-joining, weakness-embracing baptism is not only a statement of belief—although it does involve publicly renouncing the world and Satan and accepting the authority of Jesus Christ. More than a public proclamation, baptism is a memorable initiation into what William Willimon calls "another dominion," one that captivates our body as well as our mind, sticking with us as a revolutionary memory. Baptism is a liminal experience—a threshold moment that transforms self and world in ways that words can barely describe.[5]

In my congregation, for example, the rite of baptism is an unforgettable moment of drama and emotion, sometimes with tears or even sobs accompanying the otherwise mannerly performance of kneeling, confessing, getting wet, and rising. Many churches practice immersion baptism, where the believers are submerged in a baptismal font or a lake. In those settings baptism might be an outdoor experience that links our attachment to Christ with the wonder of the creation—particularly the beauty and the risk associated with bodies of water: creeks, rivers, ponds, lakes, oceans. Whether accompanied by emotion or not, the experience of rising to new life and being welcomed into the church is an irreplaceable and unrepeatable moment in the Christian life. Because of this, the church needs to make sure that an understanding of their baptism becomes part of the experience of believers.

Anabaptists have insisted on baptizing only adults, offering it as well to those whose baptism took place without conscious choice or beyond personal memory. For mainline Protestants and Catholics, confirmation has also provided a meaningful way for new believers to own their baptism. However it happens, the church must be clear about the serious consequences of baptism; it is a radical departure from convention and normalcy, the beginning of the resurrection life of defenselessness and reconciliation that is intrinsic to membership in the church.

If we are to remember who we are as God's holy people, gathered vulnerably from the broken and disabled world, we must find ways to recall the vows we made and the resurrection we experienced at baptism. By making the baptism of new members a regular feature of worship, and by inviting the congregation to participate in affirming and supporting the commitments of the baptismal class, the church can cultivate the memory and empowerment of baptism. Many congregations incorporate regular covenant renewal ceremonies into their worship life. These are occasions for baptized members to remember and reaffirm their baptismal vows as well as to pledge mutual support to one another in the ongoing burial of the old self and rebirth of the new creation that characterizes life in Christ.

Some Lutheran churches have a tradition of pouring water from a pitcher into a basin as a weekly worship ritual that encourages members to remember their baptism. A few years ago I participated in such a ceremony of covenant renewal in which participants gathered around basins of water asking for prayer and support and vowing again to renounce the dominion of sin while dipping our fingers in the water and making the sign of the cross on one another's forehead. For me, this experience recalled in powerful ways my own baptism decades earlier and joined my present struggle for faithfulness with the memory of past hopes and promises.

Baptism and the new humanity

Nothing less than the death and rebirth represented in baptism can prepare us for the world that the church sees God bringing about. Nothing less than radical grace, radical reorientation, and radical discipleship can make us part of what John Howard Yoder calls the "new interethnic social reality" that God is bringing about in the world through the witness of the church.[6]

David Morrow, in his account of reconciliation with former enemy Doroteo Rivera confirms the centrality of baptism in his new relationship with Doroteo. In the process of considering Doroteo's story and coming to see him in a new light, David witnessed Doroteo's baptism in the Gulf of Mexico. This event took place at about the same time that Morrow was considering becoming a pastor in the Mennonite church. As a Presbyterian, he had been baptized as a child, and so he requested believers baptism from his pastor. Morrow's baptism in the Gulf of Mexico took place at the same beach where Doroteo Rivera had been baptized six months earlier. He writes: "My own rebirth in Christ had occurred fifteen years earlier. Yet, as I rose out of the baptismal waters, I felt I had new life, a new opportunity for something."[7] That something turned out to be reconciliation with a former enemy and the eventual beginning of a Hispanic congregation, pastored by Doroteo Rivera, at the Warden Mennonite Church in Oregon where David was a pastor.

How then do we face the rift between the new humanity that we can see in baptism and the blindness of violence and prejudice that still surrounds us? How do we proclaim in both word and deed the triumph of the new creation over divisions and privileges of ethnicity, race, gender, class, sexuality, nationality, or ability that still remain? First, we need to remember that the new creation is not something we create by ourselves, but rather a gift received in baptism. As Yoder observes, common expressions such as *equality* and *human rights* are evidence that this gift is being received both within and beyond the church. Paul's claim that in Christ "there is no longer Jew or Greek, there is no longer slave or free, there is no longer male and female," is already being fulfilled (Galatians 3:27-29). Baptism does not make these things happen, but it enables us to see the fuller picture of God's plan for the world.[8]

Second, baptism also prepares our bodies for the emerging new creation—this new, inclusive society of restored relationships. In baptism we are being prepared to give up not only the selfishness that lies behind sins of greed, jealousy, adultery, pride, hatred, but also the selfishness that prevents us from challenging our comfort living with the dehumanizing habits of power and prejudice—whether as perpetrators, victims, or passive supporters of the status quo. We are being prepared to stand with those who suffer, even at the cost of our own comfort and affluence.

But although it might include speaking about rights, such a stand must go beyond demanding and protecting rights.[9] Demanding my rights or that of another can only get us so far; at some point it may even conflict with the full acceptance of the new humanity proclaimed in baptism. For example, rights talk has a difficult time coping with the messy and anxious social realities that emerge when a community begins to accept the gift of an anti-racist, interethnic vision. Can a focus on rights help a white man who worries that affirmative action is an obstacle to getting his dream job? Emphasizing rights may not necessarily help people face their own racism. Talking about rights may not help us listen more carefully to one another as we discuss how long-standing and valued traditions undermine the church's welcome. Discussions about church music, for example, can easily degenerate into battles over the right to sing in a particular style. Budget discussions can get focused around the division of resources between programs for youth or those in retirement. Such examples suggest that the demand for rights may be inadequate to deal with the continuing reality of sin.

Without denying the worth of social struggles framed in terms of rights, I suggest that when baptized Christians properly remember their experience of burial and rebirth, they may cope more effectively with the pain, loss, fear, and discouragement associated with struggles for social justice. Living in a renewed reality is disconcerting at first. We may not yet be able to greet one another with gentleness as brothers and sisters, and with the full delight in God's amazing good creation that the work of Jesus Christ has made possible for us.[10] We may be fearful of sitting down with strangers, especially those who challenge our comfort, our habits, or our cross-cultural language skills.

But these unnerving and sometimes terrifying experiences of disorder are not unfamiliar to anyone baptized into the passion of Christ. In baptism, we have been prepared to face death itself, as well as experiences that seem like death, in the hope of resurrection. In baptism, we have been joined with Christ and the company of saints and are learning to "be subject to one another out of reverence for Christ" (Ephesians 5:21).

Baptism and uncoupling

Subjection to one another is a mark of the believing community that makes a true life of freedom and renewed sight possible. In fact, believers baptism can be understood as an act of "striking at yourself," to use the language of Slovenian philosopher Slavoj Žižek.[11] "Striking at yourself" is the renouncing of familiar and comfortable networks of security, such as family and nationality, in order to form new, more just, associations. Žižek gets the image from a popular film where a captured protagonist voluntarily shoots himself and his captured buddy in the foot, signaling his own willingness to endure pain or die, thereby destroying the captors' power over their lives. When we are willing to die to self, we also are liberated from enslaving networks and structures.

For Žižek a feature of normal selfhood is our attachment to systems, memories, and habits within which we experience comfort and identity—relationships that help us know who we are. There is no such thing as myself by myself, without affiliation or loyalty, much as this fantasy has gripped the modern West. We are naturally dependent on those closest at hand—the nearest and dearest—for comfort and survival. The family, the tribe, and the nation are examples of systems that typically strengthen our fragile experience of security, of being connected with what is familiar and like-minded, of being propped up. Yet, at the same time, these very structures entangle us in obligations and constraints and laws that enslave us and blind us to the world of truth and freedom—of true humanity. The family that supports us also limits us. Ethnic communities both make us feel at home and alienate us from so-called nonethnic friends.

The church's long twilight struggle against racism surely reminds us of these truths. Although the church has from its beginning proclaimed itself to be a community that transcends language, race, ethnicity, and gender, over the centuries congregations and denominations have too often become identified with particular races and groups. This is why Sunday morning worship in North America is still one of our society's most segregated activities. We feel most comfortable with people like ourselves, and we feel safest when we are surrounded by people with whom we share ties of family and culture, even while we are worshipping the God who created the diversity of our species.

Self-renunciation involves uncoupling from such affiliations: the groups and laws and systems in which we live and move and have our being—systems on which we rely for predictability and security but which also undermine our capacity to truly know and love our neighbors. According to Žižek, this act of Christian uncoupling is an "active work of love" which necessarily leads to the creation of an alternative community.[12]

Žižek understands a dimension of the universe's grain that should be apparent to Christians but that we often miss. True freedom is not a matter of individual autonomy but rather of social identity. We must choose which community of affiliation will be the primary home for our struggling and divided selves. Who and what will we first and finally serve? Will it be our occupational community? The nation? The family? The mall? The marketplace? Or will it be the people of God who have come out of great tribulation and washed their robes in the blood of the Lamb, people drawn from every tribe and nation (Revelation 7:14)?

Attachment and identity are matters of life and death, of fear and courage, as can be seen from tragic events that unfolded a few years ago in the community of Lima, Ohio, near where I live. While the police were conducting a drug raid on a house suspected of containing a dangerous drug dealer, one of the policemen shot and killed an unarmed young woman, Tarika Wilson, and critically wounded the one-year-old son she was holding.

This tragedy was amplified as part of the symbolic order of American racism: the shooter was white; the young woman was black. Those who identified with the young woman tended to see the police raid as unjustified, especially given the clear signs that there were children in the house. They saw it as an example of the unrestrained violence associated with a white racist power structure. Those who identified with the police officer saw him as just doing his job and sympathized with his split-second decision to defend himself against a perceived threat.

As the community struggled to overcome the racial polarization that this horrific event brought to light, the police officer was charged with negligent homicide and negligent assault, brought to trial, and cleared of the charges. During his trial, the police officer described the circumstances he found himself in. He was approaching a darkened stairway with his gun in automatic mode and as he began to ascend the stairway, he saw a human figure emerging from the doorway at the top of the stairs. When gunshots rang out, the officer felt sure he was under attack and fired a three-round burst at the figure, which turned out to be a young woman holding a baby, rather than a drug dealer firing a weapon. The gunshots he heard turned out to be other police officers in the basement shooting at threatening dogs.

Perhaps what is most significant about this story and its aftermath is the power of fear that drove both the events leading to the tragedy and the rise in racial tensions in the surrounding community afterwards. The police officer who fired the shots that killed the young woman described his experience of being trapped between retreating—which could have put the officer behind him at risk—and firing at the apparent source of deadly gunfire: "I could have stayed there and got killed which was not an option in my mind."[13] The newspaper account says that the officer's voice cracked as he said this. The police officers that broke into the house were quite obviously all overcome by great fear, even though they were carrying automatic weapons. The police were afraid of the pit bull dogs in the basement of the house, they were afraid of the dangerous drug dealer they assumed was in the house, and they were afraid of the gunshots that they heard.

In the days following these events it became clear that many people in the neighborhood and surrounding city were afraid. Some were afraid of the police, who they perceived to be reckless in their use of violent force and racially prejudiced in their enforcement of drug laws. Some people were afraid of neighborhoods like the one Tarika Wilson lived in—full of poverty, crime, drug-dealing, and violence.

These events are a profound reminder of the complexity and power of the sin that surrounds us. The police officer's statement that being killed "was not an option in my mind," is only the most visible reminder that the fear of death lies at the root of so much sin. This fear is experienced as natural and is the basis of social order in the modern state.[14] We are fearful, so we grant to agents of the state, such as police officers, the power over life and death, so that we can feel safe. We assume that fear of weapons or punishment will stop our enemies from harming us. We are defined by our social roles: either we identify with the powers of the state or we feel victimized by those powers. We need to be uncoupled from such social roles in order to regard all the players in this tragic drama with love, respect, and the hope of salvation.

The good news of the gospel is that baptized believers can in fact live without the fear of death and neighbor that grounds so much of our current political and civic life. My friend Lynn Miller tells the story of how he and his wife, Linda, were mugged by an armed robber on their way to church. After demonstrating that they had very little money, Linda invited the robber to come to church with them and then started walking away. This refusal to demonstrate fear of deadly weapons, an act of courage, rattled the assailant who quickly put his gun away and ran off.

Our security does not need to be defined by the apparatus of punishment and death that is associated with modern state institutions of service such as the military or police. The willingness of soldiers and police officers to risk their lives to protect their neighbors is laudable, perhaps drawing near to the great love Jesus described—willing to lay down life for friends. Yet, even though such self-risk may draw near to the kingdom, its reliance on the threat of violence remains outside God's peaceable reign, outside the perfection of Christ.[15] The self-denial to which Christians are committed is defined not only by the willingness to die, but also by the respect for all life and refusal to destroy it, which Jesus taught and exemplified.

Baptism and defenselessness

Baptism leads to a self that is defenseless by the standards of our society, yet secure in the love and power of God. Such defenseless Christian love was most dramatically visible in the story of the West Nickel Mines Amish School and its confrontation with a killer, mentioned in chapter 1. After a mentally disturbed man entered the school on October 2, 2006, telling the boys to leave and the girls to line up against the wall, thirteen year old Marian Fisher said to the gunman: "Shoot me first." She was echoed by a younger sister, who said, "Shoot me second."

These entreaties did not stop the gunman, but he did ask the girls to pray for him before he began shooting at the girls, killing five and seriously injuring five others.[16] Much of the published commentary about this incident focuses on the forgiveness the Amish community showed toward the killer and his family—a persuasive witness that forgiveness is not only a Christ-like response to injury and loss, but also a deeply human response full of healing and hope for those who grieve, as well as those who feel guilt. But a more important aspect of the story is Marian's willingness to offer up her own life, an act of defenseless courage that took from the killer the power he presumed to have over her.

The words of Marian Fisher, "Shoot me first," were a request that gave a script for her younger sister to follow: "Shoot me second." Most accounts assume that Marian was trying to prevent the killer from harming the others by delaying his actions or even satisfying his thirst for violence. True as these assumptions may be, the words of the Fisher sisters are also the words of human beings who have become self-assured in their lives—lives that they knew they had received from God, lives that they were empowered to give. These were girls who had internalized the spiritual habits of their community to the extent that they instinctively knew how to offer as an act of love and courage what the gunman sought to take from them by force. By embracing defenselessness, they accomplished in the gospel sense what Žižek describes in the psychoanalytic sense: they were striking at themselves, giving up the self for the other, thereby becoming fully human, fully free. By emptying themselves in the manner of Jesus Christ, they were exalted, as the Christ hymn in Philippians describes (Philippians 2:6-11).

In contrast, the actions of the killer, Charles Roberts, reveal a man who had lost control of his own actions, a man who confessed in the note he left behind that he was filled with hate and unimaginable emptiness. Roberts was not in charge of himself or of the events that unfolded in the West Nickel Mines schoolhouse. He was governed by vengeance (for the loss of his own daughter), by some apparent form of sexual addiction, and by the forces of death.

Perhaps because Charles Roberts first of all experienced himself as a victim, as someone who had not been fairly treated by God, he was unable to retain the humanity that might have enabled him to resist the tyranny of vengeance.

Baptism and occupation

Returning to the scene of Tarika Wilson's death, we might ask what it means to be a police officer who carries a gun and who is prepared to kill in order to save his life or that of his partners. On the one hand, the service offered by the police in our communities is often self-sacrificial, engaging in risky confrontations, conflict resolution, and law enforcement, for the sake of community peace and order. Yet, the occupation of police officer—at least as practiced in the United States—presumes that deadly force is sometimes necessary to the job. The death of Tarika Wilson is a tragic example of the potential consequences of such an occupational identity.

Such an example points to a larger decision that all of us must make, whatever our occupation or station in life. When an occupation names us as people who must be prepared to harm ourselves or others in order to do our jobs, we must recall how God has named us: beloved heirs with God's Son, Jesus Christ. As children of God we are defined by God's love for us, and by our love for our neighbors, even our enemies. When we face the choice that confronted that officer—kill or be killed—we can respond in freedom. It is an option for us to be killed, rather than to kill, because Jesus Christ has overcome death and we do not need to live in fear and because we have already been killed and raised to life in baptism.

Likewise, perhaps less dramatically, it is an option for us to be demoted, or reprimanded, or to take a pay cut, because we have already been demoted and raised in glory. It is an option for us to lose our jobs, to be fired, or to resign our positions, because of our baptism into Jesus Christ. And it is an option for privileged people to give up power when confronted with the harmful effects of their privilege on others. Beyond law and policy, the waters of baptism prepare us to yield to one another in love, rather than to secure ourselves in fear.

Jesus Christ has called us by name. He has claimed us as his own, joint heirs of God, glorified with him, insofar as we are prepared to suffer with him (Romans 8:17). In baptism, we have been given eyes to see and ears to hear the new creation that is groaning to be born (Romans 8:19-25). In baptism we have been named as Christ's and our love for this world is no longer framed with human perspectives—nationalism, tribalism, sexism, classism, careerism, etc.—becoming instead the very love that Christ showed for the whole world. Baptism changes everything about who we are and about the world we now love as Christ loved—excessively and without partisanship. That is why baptism must in the final instance be chosen, either in believers baptism or in confirmation. Baptism does not come naturally; it reorders the priorities that govern the stations of life according to the assumptions of the blinded world and what that world thinks of as natural or necessary.

Baptized believers, therefore, can never justify themselves by saying that "I am just doing my job." Whenever our station demeans us or our neighbors; whenever our station undermines the loving respect for one another that is the gift of new sight, we must remember who we are. Because we are called by Christ, we will say no to any such practice of disrespect for creatures made in God's image. But, more importantly, we will by our everyday practices and habits affirm the goodness, beauty, and possibility that is intrinsic to the life of every creature of God. This does not mean that we overlook failure and sin or that we neglect to confront the evil and violence that continue to plague our world. As Eugene Peterson has put it, "Salvation is not escape from what is wrong, but a deep reconciling embrace of all that is wrong."[17] Peterson does not mean that we accept sin; but that we bring the power of God's love to the sin that surrounds us, overcoming evil with good.

For reflection and discussion

1. What are the emotions and feelings associated with baptisms you have witnessed?
2. How can the church best help its members remember their baptism?
3. What truths have you learned from those who are disabled or weak in the eyes of the world?
4. What are the circumstances where baptized followers of Jesus should leave their occupations?
5. In what ways does your work context fail to respect the creation? How does "being joined" with Jesus Christ in the church help you to see your work setting and those you serve differently?

Chapter 6

LOVE THE WORLD

My children have ways of expressing an infectious and delight-ful enthusiasm for life and for the world around them. When she was five years old, my daughter, Anna, was in the habit of announcing, at least once a week and sometimes several times a day, "I love everybody in the whole world!" My son Jacob's bedtime prayers are filled with gratitude for every aspect of his reality: "Thank you Jesus for my sister, Anna, and for Grandma and Grandpa and for the stars and for light switches and for machines and my mommy and daddy and our kitties and the wind and the sun and the grass and for chocolate-covered pretzels and play dough. In Jesus' name, Amen." When he is done, I think, "Yes, the world is really a wonderful place."

What these expressions signify is the childlike faith and delight we can recover in baptism when we put to death the sinful nature. Dutch Anabaptist Dirk Philips suggests that the words and deeds of children give us a glimpse of the kingdom of God, because children exhibit a certain innocence that has not yet been entirely overcome by the power of sin. He writes that "since Christ has now set the children as an example for us and said that we should become as children and humble ourselves, it follows from this . . . that children (so long as they are in [their] simplicity) are guiltless and reckoned without sin by God" and that there "still is something good in children . . . namely, the simple and unassuming and humble nature in which they please God."[1]

Joyful embrace

As we have seen, baptism demands the subjection of self, but it also introduces the delight and joy in the created world—including our fellow human beings—that is released from the grip of fear and self-protectiveness through baptism. An early Anabaptist hymn stresses this holy sequence of renunciation followed by great delight: "Christ the Lord says to us, 'Whoever follows me must bear his cross.' If we rightly hang on him, God will give us everything with him: first suffering, then joy, from which the devil cannot separate us."[2] This joy which follows the experience of burial and resurrection in baptism is not simply an inner piety but liberation to affirm in word and deed with the psalmist that "the earth is the LORD's and all that is in it" (Psalm 24:1).

This joy in the created world may seem contradictory to the injunctions found in the New Testament to separate from the world (2 Corinthians 6:17). There are at least two different dimensions of relating to the world in the New Testament. One aspect stresses the extent to which the world is God's good creation, loved by God and enjoyed by his creatures (1 Timothy 4:4). The other aspect focuses on the fallenness of the world, its captivity to overextended powers, and the resulting enslavement that human beings experience from the world (Ephesians 6:12).[3]

A post-baptismal love for the world is a love that is freed from the possessiveness and corruption of worldliness in order to truly respect and embrace the diversity and grace of God's creation. The world can only possess us when we devote our lives to pursuing it or possessing it. This is the sense in which the world is something we must avoid. But with renewed sight we are able to approach the world as a gift from God, not to be owned, controlled, or feared, but to be loved and embraced as God does, being willing to give one's life over to it, even at the risk of death.

This freedom extends to other human beings who are created in God's image and to our own bodies and ourselves. Christian freedom enables us to experience the joy of regarding "no one from a human point of view" but rather from the perspective of Christ, through whom God is "reconciling the world to himself" (2 Corinthians 5:16, 19).

I am reminded of singer, songwriter, and pastor Chuck Neufeld's account of his own desire to run through the streets proclaiming to everyone he met with great delight and enthusiasm: "You are created in the image of God!" If only people could remember this and live as if it were in fact true. Neufeld tells of challenging a violence-prone neighbor by shouting, "Stop! You are created in the image of God!" That is a message that our baptized lives should bring to every context, from the boardroom, to the household, to the classroom, to the courtroom, to the Congress. Wherever the lovely creation of God is being destroyed by greed, prejudice, addiction, possessiveness, war, and exploitation, we should be saying, "Stop! You are created in the image of God! We are created in the image of God!"

Servant leadership

Organizations that abandon traditional structures of hierarchy and labor management rely on the kind of respect for diverse gifts and perspectives that a baptismal consciousness cultivates. Such organizations have decided to "upend the pyramid" and that "you qualify to be first by putting other people first," in the words of servant leadership experts Ken Jennings and John Stahl-Wert.[4] They note that this management paradigm is rooted in Jesus' teaching that "whoever wishes to be great among you must be your servant" (Matthew 20:26). Such a posture of servanthood demands that leaders have a high regard for the people they serve. When we do not allow anyone to be reduced to a function within an organization and instead value the gifts contributed by each person, we are insisting on acknowledging the image of God in the neighbor.

My first job as a teenager was at my uncle's service station where I served as an attendant and assisted with simple car oil and filter changes. My uncle realized early on that my gifts were not mechanical, especially after an oil change where I forgot to put the new oil in before starting the car! So he put me to work writing and filing bills and other miscellaneous accounting tasks. This gesture gave validation to my greater skills with writing than with wrenches and helped me realize that there was a place in the world for the kind of work that I could do.

Another example of servant leadership comes from our local developmental disability system. Every bus that transports students and adults with developmental disabilities is required to have a bus aide to assist riders with their special needs. When an aide is unavailable because of illness or family obligation, a bus cannot transport the people. When this happens, rather than allowing dehumanizing delays and breakdowns of service, one facility manager steps in to serve as a bus aide even though this is far from his job description and involves work some might consider "beneath" him. The facility manager is a servant leader because he is more concerned with providing service to his fellow human beings than with preserving his status or doing only what is required. He thereby demonstrates his respect for the divine image in the people his organization serves.

Even when organizational habits do not respect the divine image in people, baptized workers can resist such dehumanizing structures by addressing their colleagues in a manner that extends hospitality and appreciation toward coworkers. Organizations do not necessarily reward such behavior, but baptized professionals take their cues from the coming peaceable reign of God, not the present blinded systems of the world.

Struggling creatures

Indeed, this respect for the divine image extends to the whole creation, of which we are a part. The first story of creation in Genesis reminds human beings that the earth and its non-human creatures preceded us. And while humanity may presume to be the crown of God's creation, we are only first because we came last, after everything else had been established. Human life was created amidst the biological and ecological processes God had already spoken into existence. Humans were made from the dust of the earth, and, we are reminded, "to dust we shall return" (Genesis 3:19). It is quite clear from the book of Genesis that this creaturely aspect of being human—of belonging to the earth and its ecological and biological systems—is thoroughly consistent with being made in the image of God and having divine worth. In fact, it is because we are part of the evolutionary processes that we experience life as a struggle that includes suffering. We are creatures that rely on one another for sustenance in a mutually dependent ecosystem that groans for deliverance (Romans 8:22). Our own bodily fates are linked with the dance of life, including the sometimes painful and destructive embraces that link the lives of creatures sharing time and space in a material world. Summarizing the work of Holmes Ralston, Nancey Murphy writes that "the universe is not a paradise but a theater where labor and suffering drive us to make sense of things."[5]

Baptism reiterates our immersion in the creaturely and material world, as well as our capacity to exceed creatureliness. As Hans Hut puts it, "baptism is . . . the water of tribulation by which the Lord makes us clean, washes and saves us from all carnal lusts, sins and unclean works and behavior."[6] The sign of baptism encourages us to discover the life that springs forth from a submission to our creatureliness, which in fact frees us from being reduced to the desires and fears associated with bodily life. Such submission does not reject the struggle for dignity and respect, but it does reject all enslaving obsessions, especially the bondage to security and self-preservation. The most human way to participate in this struggle for life and freedom is to humbly and defenselessly offer the gifts we have been given by the Creator into the social arena in which we find ourselves.

Hans Hut clearly links believers baptism and a renewed relationship to stations or occupations. He argues that believers baptism, in which God "makes dead and then brings to life again," is a sign of the power of God "which makes a person wholly new in senses, speech and heart in all actions and conduct."[7] Such wholly renewed people are ruled by God, not by their occupations. Here Hut critiques the Protestant emphasis that everyone should remain in their occupation. Protestant reformers such as Zwingli and Calvin emphasized that the stations in which people found themselves were willed by God. "If that is so," Hut asks, "why did not Peter remain a fisherman or Matthew a tax collector? Why did Christ tell the rich young ruler to sell all that he had and give to the poor?"[8]

Believers baptism brings us into a new relationship with our humanity, our bodily existence. This new relationship does not depend on the security of a paid occupation for its sustenance. Neither is bodily existence viewed as a problem to be solved or a vulnerability to be overcome.

Rather than protect or secure our bodies—in the hopes of some kind of superhuman or imperial triumph over our bodies—we present them as a "living sacrifice, holy and acceptable to God" (Romans 12:1). In baptism, all that separates us from one another, all that inclines us to pick up a weapon or clench a fist, all that produces fear and worry and resentment and grudges and retaliation, all the sin that so easily takes over, is washed away in the cleansing flood.

We discover in baptism the full reality of the good news: in the work of Jesus Christ we have been reconciled to God and one another. In Jesus Christ all are one; there is no more male or female, Jew or Gentile, slave or free, black or white, gay or straight, red state or blue state, to elaborate on the apostle Paul's words (Galatians 3:28). We no longer regard one another from a human point of view, but from the perspective of Christ, who has reconciled us all to God (2 Corinthians 5:16). By the power of the Holy Spirit, we are transformed into the likeness of Christ so that our lives reflect the new peaceable creation that God is bringing about in the world—even amidst the blindness and folly of a warring world that has not yet seen or heard this unbelievably good news and so is still acting as if power and fear and division and hatred and guns and money rule, as if the empire is still in charge.

To remember our baptism is to remember who we are in a world that makes it easy to forget. We are Christ's, above all else.

Water can help us remember who we are. Whenever we dive into a pool and come up for air, we can recall our immersion in baptismal waters and our rising to new life. Whenever we take a shower, we can remember the baptismal waters that poured over us, washing us with the waters of repentance. Whenever we drink a glass of water, we can recall the promise of living water, offered as a gift to all who come. Whenever we see a powerful river, we can recall the prophetic promise of justice that will roll down like waters and righteousness like a mighty stream. Water helps us remember that we are "created in Christ Jesus for good works, which God prepared beforehand to be our way of life" (Ephesians 2:10). Water helps us to remember that "God so loved the world that he gave his only Son, so that everyone who believes in him may not perish but may have eternal life" (John 3:16). Water helps us to love the world that God loves, and to serve it.

For reflection and discussion

1. How have the leaders that have shaped your life regarded your gifts? Have any of these leaders modeled "servant leadership"? If so, how?
2. How does God's call lead you beyond the stations of your life, just as it did the early disciples? What in your stations or occupations presents an opportunity to follow God's call?
3. What truths have you learned from children you have known?
4. How does the present world disregard and even degrade the image of God in human beings?
5. In what ways are you able to affirm the divine image in your co-workers? Your family members? Your friends? Your neighbors?

WINE:
SERVING OTHERS

Chapter 7

GIVE TO THE CHURCH

Being baptized leads to new relationships and a life together that is based on service more than on self-advancement. These new relationships go beyond culture and class difference. They introduce us to a new economy of love that grounds our life together as God's people.

When the Holy Spirit showed up on the day of Pentecost, as described in the book of Acts, the believers began speaking in tongues, using one another's language and understanding each other in a miraculous experience of cross-cultural communication and reconciliation. For the believers, this experience of being bound to one another beyond national and cultural identity led to mission and outreach, to the baptism of three thousand new believers, and to "the breaking of bread and the prayers" (Acts 2:42). For the blind, however, this spiritual outpouring looked like the result of too much new wine.

The new wine consumed by those early believers was not the kind that leads to drunkenness, as Peter explained in Jerusalem. This wine was the Holy Spirit, poured out on everyone, men and women, young and old. And following baptism, this new wine mixed with the ordinary bread and wine of the Lord's Supper led believers to give themselves completely in service to one another. They proclaimed the gospel with boldness. They healed sick people. They ate meals together. And they sold all of their possessions and joyfully redistributed the money to those in need.

Commonwealth

In this story of the early church, the social meaning of the gospel is quite clear. Those who are saved by Jesus Christ are saved from both cultural isolation and the corrupting power of wealth. All who join the church contribute from their assets to a commonwealth that looks after everyone's needs. The writer of Acts minces no words: "No one claimed private ownership of any possessions, but everything they owned was held in common" (Acts 4:32).

Throughout church history this outcome has been repeated again and again, perhaps most visibly among monastic and other radical Christian communities such as the Hutterites and the Shakers. Less visible are the ways that the sharing of wealth and property happens among Christians who do not belong to a communalist society. Offering personal resources and property to the church for the purpose of sharing with those in need is a central feature of Christian fellowship. And property includes great gifts of skill and passion that God distributes to all, expressed in different ways at different stages of life—from the voluntary service assignments taken on by young people, to the financial resources people in their earning years are able to provide, to the ministries of the local church that elderly people are often able to support with their time and unique passions.

In my own congregation we see this when young candidates for baptism who were nurtured in the church confess their dependence on the resources of the congregation for spiritual and social development, recalling the church's involvement in their lives, thanking their faith mentors, and claiming the heritage of the church as their own. In such a context it is not surprising that they are also prepared to offer their own gifts and resources to the service of the church.

At our church, baptism leads to letting go of our possessions and extending the open hand. Lists of garden and lawn care tools, construction equipment, kitchen utensils and appliances, and other household goods available for common use show up on our church bulletin board and website. Mutual use arrangements for larger vehicles such as pickup trucks and minivans appear between members of the congregation who prefer sharing costly possessions, thereby saving on money and energy costs.

Recently, when the roof shingles on my house needed replacing, several neighbors and friends loaned us the equipment and labor necessary for the task. When they found out I needed a stereo and a TV, they brought me those as well. Those who shared roofing skills and equipment—and electronic devices—were simply extending the overwhelming support my congregation provided when, a few months earlier, about 40 people helped me move across town with my two children, under challenging circumstances and personal loss. They pitched in with moving trucks, packing skills, elbow grease for cleaning, babysitting. At the end my Sunday school class organized the production of casseroles and finger food to feed the volunteers. During those shared meals the body of Christ was not merely exchanging gifts—the hand helping the foot (1 Corinthians 12:15)—but celebrating the feast of the Lord, making Christ present in our sharing of wealth and food.

It is intriguing to consider the community of goods as practiced in Acts by the outcome that the disciples celebrate: there was not a needy person among them (Acts 4:34). What perhaps seems at first like a call for sacrifice is an experience of true social security and financial well-being. Nothing to worry about; all the needs are taken care of.

During a conversation with my friend Robert Rhodes, he told me that many North American Hutterite colonies currently possess great wealth.[1] Rhodes, who lived in a Hutterite colony for many years, said that many colonies own millions of dollars in assets and savings and are able to enjoy a rather leisurely, well-supplied, and thoroughly secure way of life. The wealth comes to them both as agri-business owners and increasingly as operators of small manufacturing firms based entirely in uncompensated labor—or at least labor that is not compensated by paychecks. They work together as co-owners and coworkers, and share together the wealth that is generated. While their fairly authoritarian and deeply patriarchal colony life is not unproblematic, the Hutterites discovered that economic sharing leads to communities where no one is needy and everyone has more than enough; in fact, most Hutterites today think of themselves as collective multi-millionaires. If what you have is mine and together we have a lot of wealth, I am rich!

So the point of community of goods is profound well-being, even though it also involves the sacrifice of personal property. Furthermore, this well-being is rooted not simply in financial security but also in deep friendship. The writer of Acts notes that the early believers were of "one heart and soul" as well as a commonwealth. The language here is apparently drawn from Greek philosophy that stresses as Aristotle did that "all is shared between friends."[2] However, in the Bible, such friendship is rooted in love for God with heart and soul (Deuteronomy 6:4-6) and, as Jesus taught, love for neighbors and even enemies. Thus, the gospel extends the well-being of friendly sharing beyond the Greek philosophical idea of a community of reciprocity to mean a community of generosity, where gifts are given without expectation of payback.[3]

Such generosity is made possible by recognizing that all we have is from God and therefore is meant to be shared.[4] Like the sun and the air, which we cannot possess, all created things were made to share for our common good.[5] We can best receive the created gifts of God, not as personal possessions, but rather as a blessing for all. Focusing on the treasure of God's infinite love enables us to empty ourselves of possessiveness and to share our wealth with others.[6] Hutterite leader Peter Riedemann put it precisely: "The more a person is attached to property and claims ownership of things, the further away he is from the fellowship of Christ, and from being in the image of God."[7]

Generous stewardship

When we see that the whole creation—including our bodies and our resources— is a gift from God to be offered in service to God's children, then we come to understand ourselves as stewards rather than owners. "When God gets us he gets our property," Milo Kaufman writes, just as "when Jesus got Peter he got Peter's boat."[8]

Thus, when the church passes an offering basket during worship it is making available again and again the opportunity to participate in what Kathryn Tanner calls an economy of grace based in unconditional giving, rather than the dominant economy of scarce hoarding based in wealth accumulation.[9] Giving to the church is a practice that both builds the church's alternative grace economy and strengthens believers' intuition of generosity—which is how they face a world blinded and shaped by scarcity and greed. When I see a homeless person on a street corner holding out a cup and asking for money, it is similar to the offering basket. I cannot easily dismiss any opportunity to give because I have been trained in church every Sunday to respond generously to that basket. A prayer that is sometimes recited in my congregation during the blessing of the offerings asks God to "take these offerings . . . as our protest against all that is evil and ugly and tyrannical, in our world and ourselves—and thus may we and others know ourselves to be blessed."[10]

Recognizing ourselves as recipients of God's generosity helps us to give generously. At the same time, the practice of giving helps us come to see ourselves as blessed by God. That is why it is a good habit to always put something in the offering basket, whether it shows up on Sunday morning in the sanctuary or on a street corner on Monday afternoon. Giving to the church helps us give to the world.

For reflection and discussion

1. How do people in your congregation share their resources with one another? What are some obstacles to such sharing?

2. What are some examples of possessiveness in the culture of your workplace? What are ways that people might act generously in your workplace?

3. How can the church help its members become more generous with their money, their time, and their gifts?

4. When people ask us for money, how can we respond in ways that reflect the generosity learned in church? When might it be better not to give money?

5. Why do most Christians not literally follow the practice of complete divestment of private property as described in Acts 4? What can we learn from Christian communities such as the Hutterites who do practice such communalism?

Chapter 8

SHARE BREAD AND WINE

It may seem that such a life of stewardship is only for heroic individuals, monastic orders, or peculiar sectarian colonies. But the good news is that anyone who seeks to follow Jesus by the power of the Holy Spirit and in the context of Christian community can experience the resurrection power of economic sharing. In Jesus' life and ministry we find the most miraculous social and economic transformation taking place around the most ordinary practices: sharing bread and drink together around a table. Whether by including sinners and social outcasts at his table, by providing wine at a wedding celebration, or by feeding five thousand people with the loaves and fishes offered by a young boy, Jesus showed that inclusive and just table fellowship is a central feature of the reign of God.

Sharing bread

John Howard Yoder says that the Lord's Supper, as instituted by Jesus, recalled for the early church not only the death of Jesus but also the life of just and generous sharing that he taught and practiced. Sharing bread around the table begins to fulfill the Jubilee expectations that Jesus had announced at the beginning of his ministry (Luke 4:18-19). Restoring land, canceling debts, and redistributing wealth were the marks of the coming Jubilee, and were now being fulfilled as people from different classes and cultures began eating together.

The early church understood breaking bread in exactly this way, according to Yoder. The texts from Acts that describe the community of goods closely link the breaking of bread with economic sharing. In Paul's letter to the Corinthians he challenges the church to overcome the social stratification that became obvious during the sharing of bread and wine, when some people were getting drunk while others were left hungry (1 Corinthians 11:21). By contrast, when Christians from different classes actually shared food equally around a table, they were demonstrating that the messianic age had arrived.[1]

Moreover, their sharing of food and drink was not merely a ceremonial sign of something else, "bread eaten together is economic sharing. Not merely symbolically, but also in fact, eating together extends to a wider circle the economic solidarity normally obtained in the family."[2] Thus the concrete practice of sharing food together—that was shaped by the Jewish Passover tradition and Jesus' own teachings and practices— is the doorway to a renewed and liberated economic community of service and giving.

Even the basic concept of tithing, which is generally understood to be the practice of giving a tenth of one's earnings to God, is rooted in the practice of sharing food. For example, the book of Deuteronomy, where it describes tithing practices, tells God's people to set aside a tithe of their crops to be brought into "the presence of the Lord your God." But this tithe is not sent away, burned on an altar, or sacrificed. Instead, the people of God are instructed to "eat the tithe of your grain, your wine, and your oil, as well as the firstlings of your herd and flock, so that you may learn to fear the LORD your God always" (Deuteronomy 14:23). During this time the tithes are also shared with the priestly class—the Levites—and with orphans and widows and resident aliens. But the practice of tithing is clearly less about philanthropy and more about sharing. People of all kinds and means gather and eat from the tithe that has been set apart for the purpose of rejoicing together and being present to God.

In our own time, when fewer and fewer meals seem to be shared around a table, this practice of gathering together with strangers and friends for a common meal—whether in church or in the household—is a basic act of economic justice and personal conversion. Surely this should not surprise us. How often have transformative conversations taken place during gatherings with friends around a table spread with food and drink? How often have we been knitted together with other believers in sharing bread and wine during the Lord's Supper? How often has a potluck offered new taste sensations as well as introduced us to new friends? Even committee meetings can be more jovial and pleasurable with the presence of food.

For the past two years, my family has participated in a cooperative farm in which sixteen families share the planting and harvesting of a large vegetable garden. For the cost of one trip to the grocery store, our shared work leads to harvests of more food than most of us know what to do with—vegetables on the doorstep, vegetables in the basement, vegetables over-flowing the kitchen counter, and boxes and jars full of vegetables for winter. We have a regular potluck meal where we share food prepared mostly from our garden; it is a delightful ritual that celebrates our discovery of abundance.

My experiences of sharing food with others lead me to question the frequency with which I consume food alone. The availability of fast food that can be eaten on the run or while driving toward an appointment undermines my commitment to sharing food with others. A busy daily schedule and a full inbox tempt me to eat lunch by myself in my office while catching up with email, rather than interacting with colleagues in the lunch room. The migration of breakfast toward a quick bowl of cereal tends to discourage shared time together with family in the morning before everyone gets out of the house. In our time and place, breaking bread with others is an increasingly radical act that we must seek to recover both in family and community life. It helps us remember that our very sustenance is a marvelous gift of God which should be celebrated together with others whose lives are bound up with ours.

Our experience of breaking bread with others should strengthen our resolve to share our wealth with those in need. Traditional prayers that express gratitude for daily bread and remember those who go without remind us of the task before Christians to spread a table for everyone, including especially those who have been excluded from their full and fair share of wealth by our stratified global economy.

Sharing wine

As we have seen from our discussion about bread, the elements of bread and wine that signify the body and blood of Christ in communion open up the door to a much larger new world that God is preparing for us. Sharing wine, which in traditional Christian communion services signifies Christ's blood poured out for us, is more complicated.

In modern times, many Christian churches have substituted grape juice for wine in communion because of the role that alcohol can play in destroying lives—whether because of drunk driving or because of the disease of alcoholism. North American Christians are right to be cautious about the use of alcohol in this way. However, to recover the full meaning of the communion meal we need to recall the more celebratory dimension of wine consumption in the biblical context and in other cultures. Since we don't typically associate grape juice with parties, we can easily forget the celebratory and transformative aspect of the Lord's Supper.

Wine was prized in ancient times as an expression of celebration and hospitality and valued because it could "release the human spirit from the power of the mind."[3] In the Bible, we find texts that affirm the social use of wine as an expression of delight and gladness: "Go, eat your bread with enjoyment, and drink your wine with a merry heart, for God has long ago approved what you do" (Ecclesiastes 9:7). Moreover, wine is valued precisely because of its capacity to "gladden the human heart" (Psalm 104:15), because of its reputation for healing (1 Timothy 5:23), and because it can be used for those who are "in bitter distress" to "forget their poverty and remember their misery no more" (Proverbs 31:6-7).

At the same time, there are Scriptures that warn against being "drunk with wine" (Ephesians 5:18) and caution leaders with important social responsibilities against drinking, because drunkenness can have a damaging impact on the poor who rely on rulers for sober judgments. Consistent with concern about the impact of alcohol on decision-making, Paul writes that leaders of the church should be "temperate" and "not a drunkard," among other things (1 Timothy 3:2-3). The apocryphal book of Sirach states the biblical vision for proper use of wine most precisely: "Wine drunk at the proper time and in moderation is rejoicing of heart and gladness of soul. Wine drunk to excess leads to bitterness of spirit, to quarrels and stumbling" (Sirach 31:28-29).

The inclusion of wine as a key element of the Christian communion ritual signifies that the gathering at the Lord's Table is not only a practice of economic sharing and mutual nourishment, but of hospitable celebration and sensual delight—Jesus himself drank wine with friends. The presence of wine is a reminder that communing with the body of Christ gladdens our spirits and opens us to God's grace.

One Mennonite congregation I visited recently offered participants the choice of either juice or wine during their celebration of the Lord's Supper. Such a practice acknowledges both the delight of wine and the discipline of abstinence.

Wine, whether taken in moderation or avoided altogether, is a reminder of the joy of celebration by the people of God gathered around food and drink. Because wine also has so much potential for harm, it reminds us of the accountability we all require in order to avoid self-destructive behavior. We need the presence of others in order to be transformed by the Spirit and also to exercise discernment (1 John 4:1).

Sanctifying bodies

None of these practical social dimensions of sharing bread and wine should detract from the holiness of the Lord's Supper—whether in beautiful formal sanctuaries or ordinary meals around the dining room table. Pilgram Marpeck stated eloquently that in such faithful practices as the Lord's Supper and other acts of practical service, the humanity of Christ continues to be present in history.[4]

In traditional Anabaptist services of communion, the relationship between sharing bread and offering service is made explicit with the ritual of footwashing that typically follows the communion meal. Believers who have just offered one another bread and juice now kneel before each other with basin and towel to pour water over each other's feet and to wipe the feet dry with a towel.[5]

A dimension of this cleansing, of course, is the experience of mutual vulnerability and dependence that is strengthened in the act of giving and receiving the washing of feet. Barriers of status, ideology, age, gender, and occupation can fall away as we become first of all servants to each other. People who serve each other with basin and towel are now prepared also to open their bank accounts to each other as they give offerings of thanksgiving. Through these practices of caring and serving associated with the Lord's Supper, the holiness of human bodies is highlighted.

In Western culture, where we have too often preferred the mind over the body, this attention to human bodies as vessels of love to be tended, washed, and served is an important reminder that our bodies are temples of the Holy Spirit. Tending to one another's bodies is one way we sanctify and serve each other as God's creation. Washing one another's feet should lead us to be concerned for the bodily health of our neighbors and to support public health practices that promote the well-being and healing of human bodies. Many Christians enter the health professions deeply shaped by this affirmation of the goodness of human bodies. Washing feet leads to all kinds of healing practices, from surgery to chiropractic, from psychotherapy to oncology. Such gifts of healing and sanctification are part of a larger economy of gift sharing that rehumanizes us.

Sharing gifts

It might be difficult for those of us immersed in a capitalist economy to grasp the social bonds that follow from gift exchanges
in the biblical setting. Stephen Long and Tripp York point out
the obligations that are attached with gifts in pre-modern gift
exchange economies: "to give a gift is to request that a gift be
given in return; to accept a gift is to commit oneself to such
an economy."[6] The obligations associated with gifts have not
entirely escaped us, of course. When we receive a gift at Christ-
mas from a friend or a coworker, we do feel some obligation to
offer a gift in return. When we tell people that we don't need
anything for a special occasion, we are in part trying to head
off the obligation that we feel to those who have bothered getting us a gift.

In fact, a good deal of so-called middle-class effort is
expended on extracting ourselves from the obligations of gift
exchanges. When I pay a teenager to care for my children in my
absence, rather than setting them up with another family, I don't
feel I have to offer to take care of that family's children. Paying
for goods and services with money, rather than offering and
receiving our resources in community helps us feel autonomous
and self-sufficient—the modern version of "freedom." But such
autonomy also destroys the potential for excess and grace, and
undermines the power of practices such as the Lord's Supper to
bind believers together in their ministries to the world. Instead,
we offer bread and juice to one another as a kind of polite ritual
that at best points toward tolerance of one another, but avoids
investment in each other's lives.

A few years ago, my wife and I decided to enter into a vehicle sharing arrangement with another family from our congregation. We had a minivan that could serve the needs of our
friends—a family of five whose only reliable transportation
was an energy efficient compact. I, on the other hand, was
attracted to the gas mileage of their compact car, because of
the frequent trips I made transporting my children to school in
another city. When our friends needed to go on lengthy trips,
they borrowed our van. When we needed an extra compact
car for energy-efficient transportation, we borrowed their car.

On one occasion, our friends wanted to take our car on a particularly long trip, offering extra compensatory gifts, such as child care and extra use of their car, which were not, however, available while they were gone. We accepted the exchange, realizing that being without the minivan for a whole week had the potential to add complexity to our lives. During that time I attended a conference in another state and was car-pooling with colleagues. My wife left town before I came back to spend time with the kids and some of her extended family at a vacation house nearly two hours away. I suddenly realized that I was going to be dropped off to a home with no cars in the driveway. The van was in Minnesota and the car was in Indiana. This is exactly the sort of situation that middle-class people try to avoid by always having a car available. When I mentioned this predicament to a colleague, we realized that she was planning to drive to Indiana the next day. She dropped me off at a gas station in Indiana half an hour away from my family and I could enjoy part of that weekend with them. In the meantime, we had a conversation on the way that we otherwise would not have had, we cut the energy consumption for our trip in half, and our friends had a delightful trip to Minnesota with our minivan.

There is nothing heroic here. But for me this story illustrates the lovely potential associated with gift-giving habits that resist the idolatry of self-sufficiency. All the people involved were shaped by communities of faith that encouraged gift exchanges over the money economy as the basic currency of social life. And we are all struggling to live our lives together in ways that resist putting price tags on our bodies and on the gifts we offer one another. When we do this, even on a modest scale, we discover a world full of surprises. In fact, we experience the closest thing to a miracle that educated twenty-first century participants in the culture of capitalism are ever likely to experience.

For reflection and discussion

1. In what ways does your congregation's practice of communion highlight the economics of sharing? How might this aspect of communion be made more explicit?

2. How can the church reclaim the celebratory aspect of the Lord's Supper?

3. How should contemporary Christians regard the consumption of wine? What are the best ways to discourage the abuse of alcohol?

4. How can you share more of your resources with others?

5. What are some of the ways that our society discourages sharing gifts with each other? What are some of the risks associated with sharing?

Chapter 9

SERVE THE WORLD

The miracle of the gift unleashed in the Lord's Supper is not only for us in the church. It is, like the mission of biblical Israel, a gift for the world. Yoder writes that "the newness of the believing community is the promise of newness on the way for the world. That in the age of the Messiah those in bondage will be freed and the hungry will be fed is also a criterion, though a distant one, for political economics beyond the circle of faith."[1] In other words, the sharing of life and wealth practiced by the church, when it is faithful, becomes a witness and a model for the surrounding society. Of course, because the church is all too often unfaithful with respect to just economic sharing among its own members, a primary task is to continue calling the church to live out the kind of stewardship found in the Bible. But ultimately that call must move beyond the congregation and be offered to the world that God is in the process of redeeming and reclaiming.

Neighborhood revitalization

An illustration of just how far-reaching and socially transformative a graceful economics can be comes from the city of Pittsburgh. During my graduate school years there, I was a member of Pittsburgh Mennonite Church where there was indeed much breaking of bread—in regular observance of the

Lord's Supper, in regular potlucks and a yearly congregational retreat with a feast of Indian food, in weekly small group gatherings, and much more. A vision that emerged from that congregation was to share with our city the skills of college students who had been nurtured in communities of stewardship that were located primarily in rural areas. Thus, in 1994 the Pittsburgh Urban Leadership Service Experience program was born. This program brought college graduates from Mennonite and other primarily Christian institutions into the city of Pittsburgh for internships at social agencies and nonprofit organizations that sought to renew the life of the city. Participants in the program shared a house and placed all remuneration from the internships into a common fund, thereby making it possible for some to serve in places that could not afford to pay. More than a hundred PULSE alumni now live in the city of Pittsburgh working as artists, musicians, educators, and organizational leaders on behalf of the reign of God. They offered their lives and skills to the city, not simply as a short-term voluntary-service assignment—which is also a valuable form of service—but as a stewardship gift of all that they are and have.

One of the many amazing projects to emerge from PULSE alumni is the Union Project. Just down the road from the PULSE house in what had been a declining neighborhood in Pittsburgh sat a beautiful but abandoned building—the former Second Presbyterian Church. The place was in an increasing state of disrepair in a neighborhood that desperately needed renewed common space. In 2001, the Union Project board bought the building with assistance from church organizations and community foundations.

In the years since, this abandoned church building has become a home for artists, community builders, and people of faith. An emergent church meets in the sanctuary that has been renovated into a community meeting hall. This sanctuary space is still full nearly every day with community events and gatherings of just about every kind imaginable. There are tenant-partners who rent office space in the building and contribute to a sustainable economy for the project. A coffee shop is being opened in cooperation with Peabody High School's culinary arts academy. The project has recently completed a successful $1.5 million capital campaign. A summer art and farmers market brings artists and farmers together with neighbors to buy and sell and admire good food and art.

The most amazing feature of the Union Project is its stained glass window repair project. After assessing the damage of the stained glass windows and realizing that there were no funds to pay a contractor to restore them, the project leaders decided to offer stained glass restoration classes to the community. Their stained glass windows could be used as a laboratory for students who were learning stained glass techniques. Over a hundred people have now taken these classes and all the windows are now restored. Consequently, they are exploring the idea of a stained glass cooperative. This project is a beautiful example of what is possible when creative and faithful Christians think outside the highly restrictive economy of consumption and personal ownership and instead seek to build economies of gift-giving and communally shared wisdom, skill, and service.[2]

It is most fitting that in this community of renewal called the Union Project a weekly ritual is the Friday afternoon happy hour, serving food and wine to neighbors and friends from a bar crafted from the church's altar. The dreams and visions of young men and women in Pittsburgh revitalized an entire neighborhood through the fairly simple conviction that when people are brought together around shared food and shared resources, the reign of God appears among us, by the grace and power of God.

Vocational giving

Graceful economics applies not only to imaginative young people reversing a declining neighborhood. During my congregation's midweek shared meal, we are treated to the faith stories of those who have experienced God's generosity in their own lives and practices. Recently, we heard that several retired women in our congregation were making a quilt to be the featured quilt for our area Mennonite Relief Sale. Each of them described the contribution they made to the quilt, from the design, to fabric selection, to piecing the fabric, to the actual moment of quilting. The congregation was invited to contribute donations toward the cost of the materials. When the quilt is sold at the relief sale, it is quite possible that it will be immediately donated back for resale, as has happened in years past. In the loving production of this quilt and thousands like it each year throughout North America, the gifts of many different members of Christ's body—from craft production to community organizing to event coordination and market auctioneering—are parlayed into an alternative economic community. It is a community where offering of oneself to the world is experienced as an occasion for celebration and delight, rather than charity or philanthropy (or grudging submission to a social welfare system based on taxes).

While offering charity and paying taxes are good things to do, they presume the validity of our current economic system, which assumes that the world is organized around private property, from which people decide how much to give away. Grace-based economies, on the other hand, assume that all we have is from God. The question is not how much to give away, but rather how much we need to invest in ourselves. In a grace-based economy, we are constantly looking for ways to give away the time, money, and strength that we have received from God, reserving for ourselves only what we need to be renewed and sustained in our lives.

Another dramatic example of such grace-based economics is the decision of Dave and Karen Mast to sell their house and move into a travel trailer, in which they travel around the country, offering their service to the volunteer ministries of the church, such as church camps, retreat centers, and relief support. Dave, who is fifty-one, continues to work as an airline pilot while joining Karen, forty-eight, in volunteer service for two to three days at a time between flight schedules.[3]

Dave and Karen Mast are experiencing the blessings of living with enough. Lynn Miller urges us to consider receiving such blessings, rather than consuming all we can afford. Because the surrounding consumer culture is designed to make us spend money on things we don't need and sometimes don't even want, Miller emphasizes how important it is to list all those goods and services that we need to be happy. The point is not to deprive ourselves but rather to discover what we need in order to be content. Thinking about this question is already the first step of liberation from consumer culture, which gains much of its leverage by discouraging us to think about what and why we buy.[4]

Reducing our spending to purchase only enough for our happiness frees our money to be given away. Miller urges Christians to think of their retirement plans in terms of this paradigm of living with enough. Once we have established how much we need in order to live well in retirement, and once we have developed a plan for how to achieve that, the question then becomes: To whom or what should we devote our excess money? Miller advocates giving away the excess immediately "because people need it now," and calls this "vocational giving." The key to such a radical approach to money is being able to define "enough." As Miller puts it, "if you can't tell me how much is enough, you will never have enough."[5]

Whether we are senior college students beginning to think about applying for our first full-time professional job or whether we are senior citizens, considering how to contribute our gifts during the greater leisure of retirement, remembering our baptism into Christ should help us with the decision. Our regular participation in the Lord's Supper and other practices of service should help us remember what it means to serve God by serving others.

Public welfare and taxes

The grace-based economy of generosity just described, found throughout the history of Israel and the church, can also be discovered in the so-called secular public sphere, even when Jesus Christ is not being explicitly proclaimed. Each autumn, my wife, Carrie, and I make a pilgrimage to her former employer: Marimor Industries in Lima, Ohio. It is a company run by the local county board of developmental disabilities (DD) to employ people whose gifts are not well-received in a marketplace dominated by efficiency. Marimor is supported by a tax levy that needs to be renewed every four years, so the DD board organizes a yearly chicken barbecue each year to raise money for the levy campaign.

Carrie and I arrive at the Marimor complex in the late forenoon and join at least fifty volunteers who are working in assembly lines filling up take-out boxes with chicken, applesauce, potatoes, rolls, and dinnerware. Behind the building a traveling chicken barbecue operation is well underway as the smoke rises and pleasing odors drift toward us. Our job is to pick up a trunkload of barbecued chicken meals that we will transport around town to organizations that have purchased them for lunch. Throughout the town, other volunteers like us are also distributing these meals on wheels and collecting money for the tax levy fund. Radio stations remind listeners that today they can buy chicken barbecue for lunch while signs on shop windows and advertisements in the local newspapers announce the event. Many people with a variety of gifts and resources devote an enormous amount of effort and energy toward the goal of making room for people with disabilities in the marketplace.

This event might be less than biblical grace-based economics; but it is a step in that direction. On the one hand are people who support Marimor and people with disabilities with money and resources towards the levy promotion fund. On the other hand, the money raised—using the services of a for-profit barbecue company—promotes a levy that will raise taxes even for people who do not wish to fund Marimor. The delight of voluntary service coexists with the redistributive justice of coercive taxation and the entrepreneurial energy of profit. Still, it turns out that people with disabilities continue to receive service and to offer their gifts in Allen County, Ohio. There is some coercion and profit involved, but in the end there is enough grace and generosity to sustain space for those who might otherwise be "outsiders" and for volunteers to change the meaning of paying taxes from an act of grudging obedience to a cheerful act of generosity toward others.

The Marimor fundraising project raises the question: What if taxes were no longer simply a certainty associated with death but an opportunity for joyful sacrifice on behalf of the society that we are part of? What if people could come to experience the pleasure of the tithe described in Leviticus? Because taxes are coerced, it is unlikely that people will be able to see them that way without the development of giving habits that are cultivated by communities such as the church. All too often, however, the church inveighs against taxes, preferring the opportunity to give voluntarily to the obligation to give lawfully. While it is true that public goods are altogether too often squandered and misused—especially in the name of such idolatrous projects as "homeland security" and "national defense"—it is also true that the commitment to the common good that is associated with taxes is more closely aligned with the liberation of the gospel than is the valorization of private wealth associated with capitalism. Sharing, redistribution, sacrifice, and giving are all terms or phrases that characterize the biblical understanding of economic life in direct contradiction to the capitalist priority of "storing up treasures" for ourselves (Luke 12:21). Paying taxes, like working a job, can be seen as an opportunity to identify ourselves with those dimensions of the cultural orders that are more closely aligned with the way of Jesus—the way of service.

Giving our gifts of occupational skill or financial wealth should be done as acts of what John Howard Yoder called revolutionary subordination: "the acceptance of an order, as it exists, but with new meaning given to it by the fact that one's acceptance of it is willing and meaningfully motivated."[6]

For reflection and discussion

1. What opportunities for revitalization and voluntary service exist in your neighborhood? Why is it difficult to incorporate voluntary service into daily life?

2. How should Christians view their tax obligations? Should we be advocating an increase in taxes in order to make more social services available to our neighbors or should we argue for a reduction of taxes in order to strengthen business and entrepreneurship?

3. What are some of the things that you need to be content? What possessions of yours are not required for contentment?

4. How should retirement planning within the calling of Christ differ from typical approaches to retirement?

5. How can church members model and encourage greater generosity in our society?

WE:
LIVING IN COMMUNITY

Chapter 10

YIELD TO THE CHURCH

When baptized people begin to share life together in new relationships based on service and love, a new community starts to take shape. This community is the church of Jesus Christ, which frees us to live in hope and empowers us to make peace. We discover that we are not alone, that our lives are in God's hands and with God's people.

During a recent personal crisis, I called a close friend and pastor in another state and asked for his wisdom and guidance. This brother in Christ spent the next six months on the phone with me nearly every day offering biblical counsel and urging me at every moment to follow Christ's way of peace and yieldedness rather than to give in to fear, anger, and the temptation to fight. When I heard his voice, I knew he spoke the truth—my fears and anxieties were calmed, and I was strengthened in faith and hope. However, resting in the hope of Christ required that I continue to talk with this friend and brother. Sometimes I could make it for several days without phoning him, while at other times my rest was interrupted after a few hours. The gifts of pastoral and priestly wisdom that I received from this brother were indispensable for my spiritual, emotional, and physical well-being during this most challenging time of my life.

Truth telling

This personal experience illustrates how community life can change us for the better and help us resist bad ideas or impulses. As individuals, we are bombarded with persuasive messages and peer pressure from the culture around us. Assumptions about appropriate occupational choices, the right life partner, reasonable family arrangements, efficient management practices, wise budgeting, and smart retirement planning swirl around us and constrain our decision-making. Television commercials and Internet messages shape our desires and consumption practices.[1]

Increasingly our sense of self and the world is shaped by screens, especially computer screens which glow in front of many of us for most of our working hours. They organize our self-understandings and relationships to others through shallow, software-based environments of email, instant messaging, spreadsheets, word processors, and media programs.[2] We are subject, in other words, to many communities of meaning and authority: our families, our work, branding or marketing, sports teams, the nation, the Kiwanis Club, and a host of other groups with which we identify.

For Christians, navigating among these competing communities of meaning is not an individual project but one oriented by life together in the primary community of faith—the body of Christ. The church with whom we worship on Sunday is with us at work on Monday. A passage in the book of Ephesians states it well: "We must no longer be children, tossed to and fro and blown about by every wind of doctrine, by people's trickery, by their craftiness in deceitful scheming" (Ephesians 4:14). The writer goes on to emphasize that members of Christ grow up into Christ by "speaking the truth in love" (Ephesians 4:15) to one another. We must speak to one another, and we must do so in love, otherwise we will not be truthful.[3] When we speak out of genuine love for one another we can resist together the habits of falsehood and trendiness that so easily overtake us.

Unfortunately, this kind of communication is not always present; many people have experienced religious communities as oppressive. They have sometimes concluded that to be free they must leave the church behind—to treat the church like every other decision about consumption, based on customer satisfaction rather than Christian obedience. But the community of faith that lovingly empowers believers to live in freedom is not an authoritarian institution built around defensive rules and doctrines nor is it a self-actualizing therapeutic spiritual service provider.

The practices stressed in the book of Ephesians focus on concern for both the unity of the body and the dignity of each member of the body. Communication here cannot mean scolding or treating a member as a threat to the institution. Instead, the members of the body discipline each other, bear with one another, seek unity together, and strengthen the bond of peace.

A few years ago, I struggled with a workload that had become overwhelming because I had said yes to more responsibilities than I could handle. Bewildered and paralyzed, I asked for help from colleagues who were most directly involved with my daily schedule. Fortunately for me, they were also members of the body of Christ, who knew me as a brother and not just as a coworker. We met at the academic dean's house, around a pot of soup. The discussion was pointed, with questions that focused on how I had gotten myself into this mess. This was an opportunity for truth telling, for honest discussion of who I was and what my gifts were. It also included painful acknowledgements of areas where I had not succeeded. And I shared my frustrations with some of my colleagues' decisions, which I felt had affected me negatively. This honest mutual sharing led to a discovery and affirmation of a healthy way forward for me.

True friendship

The calling of Christ is more than going to church, joining the church, or even keeping all the church's rules. I am advocating a baptism-empowered submission to brothers and sisters in Christ who have discovered in one another the delight and liberty of true friendship. Such honest and truthful accountability will normally involve a discernment group drawn from friends in Christ who are not part of the work setting (unlike my own setting). But such habits of mutually encouraging communication might also lead to practices of gift-discovery and affirmation in the workplace. The crucial element here is a community of faith and friendship that grounds all of one's actions and decisions and that provides guidance about how to act in every communal setting.

David Matzko McCarthy, in his book *The Good Life*, describes such deep and true friendship by comparing it to the more superficial forms of friendliness in contemporary life. According to McCarthy, American culture encourages me to see the neighbor primarily as a means to my own ends, to be treated politely and perhaps kindly, so long as there is an apparent benefit for me in the relationship.[4]

In contrast with mere friendliness, friendship is a disruptive and transformative relationship based in a common vision of what is good and true. True friends have discovered a life-changing relationship that exceeds the pragmatic friendliness pervading most workplaces. "They start to live, struggle, and move forward side by side with the same way of envisioning the future. Friends conspire. They plan. They want to make a difference. They seek a goal that is beyond each and attainable only together. Together they are able to imagine a different kind of world, and together they are able to act in it."[5]

McCarthy observes that such friendships are often tempted to withdraw or to remain closed against outsiders. But he encourages friends to resist this temptation and to extend the circle to others who may share the vision.

Yieldedness to the body of Christ can take place when the church is visible among such a hospitable community of friends. Thus there is a dimension of smallness or intimacy that is required for true submission or discipline to take place. Large church congregations are not likely to function in this way, although congregations may very well include many smaller communities of friendship and accountability.

Amish writer David Kline highlights the ways in which successful deep, accountable communities have a local focus. He remembers coming home to his Amish community from conscientious objector service in a city hospital during the Vietnam War and realizing that all of his role models and heroes and mentors were "neighbors rather than entertainment celebrities." He notes that one reason small towns and markets in Amish Country are thriving, even though there is a Wal-Mart ten miles away, is "because of the horse."[6] By limiting most of their transportation to locations within driving distance of horse and buggy, Amish communities have strengthened their local economies, along with the deeper and longer-term relationships associated with such close-at-hand commerce. Those of us who seek disruptive friendship rather than merely convenient friendliness must evaluate how technologies such as cars and computers present obstacles to deep and accountable forms of community.

If modern technologies of communication and transportation undermine the ties that bind communities together, there are also practices that can help sustain such ties. One such practice by which the church cultivates the habits of mind and body that strengthen the mutual subjection of friends is singing together, the focus of the following chapter.

For reflection and discussion

1. Recall challenging times in your life when you experienced the support of friends and fellow church members or for which you wish there had been stronger community support.

2. Who are the people in your circle of friends with whom you share "friendship" rather than merely "friendliness"? If you do not have such a circle, what have been some of the obstacles to forming one?

3. What are the communities of meaning that compete with the church for loyalty and time in our setting? How can we insist on the priority of the church?

4. What are the forms of church community that provide direction to your life? How can the church do more to provide direction?

5. What are some of the dangers associated with close community relationships of the kind advocated in this chapter?

Chapter 11

SING TOGETHER

The writer to the Ephesians admonishes his audience to "be subject to one another out of reverence for Christ." Before this instruction, however, is the call to sing together: "Do not get drunk with wine, for that is debauchery; but be filled with the Spirit, as you sing psalms and hymns and spiritual songs among yourselves, singing and making melody to the Lord in your hearts, giving thanks to God the Father at all times and for everything in the name of our Lord Jesus Christ" (Ephesians 5:18-21).

Singing and yieldedness

David Ford argues that the way singing shows up before subjection in the Ephesians 5 text is not accidental. That is because by singing together participants learn what it means to be subject without being dominated.[1] To sing together is to learn how to yield to one another, to be attentive to one another, to recognize the gifts of another, to be moved by another, and to be responsive to the expression of another. Singing together is crucial for life together.

When I think of the power of music to subject us, the image that comes immediately to my mind is of the person in the car next to mine pumping loud music through subwoofers that shake his car and mine. His entire body moves in response to the music, arms flying and head pumping up and down.

He seems to have yielded completely to the sounds coming through an electronic device, or to the digital codes that were mass-produced to create such an experience. Such subjection is often experienced as freedom and liberation, whether in a shaking car or on a dance floor. While it is clear that some musical experiences can assist people in liberation, and even help form movements for social change, other musical practices subject listeners to nihilism, sexual slavery, death, and destruction. Music is not only self-expressive art, but also a human activity that shapes what is going on in our minds and in our relationships. Unfortunately, a good deal of popular music tends to be something we purchase and enjoy as individuals, often through earpieces that cut us off from the people around us. The sort of music-making I'm calling for is social and helps us to build communities of friendship and attentiveness.

In church, when people sing together, they blend their voices, sometimes harmoniously, sometimes not. They listen to one another, and to a chorister, an organist, or a worship band in order to know how fast or slow to sing, how loudly or quietly. They follow words and musical notation on a page or a screen, making the words and notes their own. In Christian congregations the social experience of singing is given over to the praise of God, "making melody to the Lord." It offers a profound integration of community, transcendence, offering, and thanksgiving.

In their study of the singing experiences of Mennonites, Marlene Kropf and Kenneth Nafziger confirm this integration of heaven and earth in the singing, and say that singing should properly be thought of as sacramental, as a practice that "creates the body of Christ."[2] Citing Karl Barth's comment that "the community which does not sing is not the community," they explore the manifold ways in which Mennonites have discovered singing to be a necessary foundation of community life. The people they interviewed described the multiple layers of connectedness they experience as they sing. Singing brings together body and spirit and envelops the whole person in the community of praise.[3]

Among the striking comments they collected is one from Lee Snyder confirming the marvelous sensuality of blended voices: "Basses and tenors singing with sopranos and altos—that's a very sensuous thing. Sometimes that is what I'm thinking about when I'm singing. When I listen to wonderful voices around me, I am always curious who is singing. I try not to be rude and turn around and look. It's very mesmerizing; it's very attractive, and a lot like sexual attraction."[4] This acknowledgment of sanctified *eros* suggests that singing can shape even the character of the passions and desires that we feel for one another, toward the world, and toward God. Moreover, such a delight in the body—both the body of Christ and the bodies that are its members—makes the praise of God more than a rational affirmation. Doxological singing becomes a holy offering of our bodies to one another and to God in an expression of gratitude that melds ecstasy and praise.

Music and memory

Singing knits the body of Christ together by cultivating mutual subjection in the full-bodied praise of the Creator. But it also connects us to memory, both the memory of the distant past and the recent past. Rowan Williams points out that in singing psalms and hymns Christian congregations not only express the unity of our faith, despite ongoing division, but also establish our relationship to the communion of saints throughout history. By singing hymns and reciting Scripture together, we believers give ourselves over to a language that we do not control, speech and rhythms from other times and places, and a memory of witness that transcends our own narrow perspective.[5] Thus singing, like reading the Bible, is a spiritual discipline. These practices challenge "the assumption that I—my conscious, willing ego—stand at the center of all patterns of meaning."[6]

At the same time, singing has an impact even on our short-term memory enabling us to carry the body of Christ with us into the marketplace, providing rhythms and cadences and words and voices in our heads that can shape our responses to everyday tasks and crises. A member of our congregation recently related that when she travels the road to a very challenging administrative job each morning she is accompanied by the songs we had sung the previous Sunday; the memory of the music gives her courage and perspective for the day ahead.

I have a vivid memory from my childhood of walking down the lane to catch a ride to school past the town feed mill where my great-uncle Paul Stutzman worked. Even though I was hundreds of yards away from the mill, I could hear him whistling the songs we had sung together on Sunday in church. I have never heard anyone whistle as cheerfully or as loudly—a lovely sound that outstripped the sound of feed bags thrown into pickup trucks, of corn rustling into a wagon, of the growling of a noisy tractor. I also have early memories of my mother singing while doing the dishes, washing the laundry, cleaning the house, weeding the garden, putting away corn. "Count your many blessings, name them one by one," she sang over and over again. "Blessed assurance, Jesus is mine." For myself, very little happens in an ordinary day without an old hymn coming to mind. My great-uncle Paul and my mother know how to carry the body of Christ with them into their daily lives—by praising God in the words and music of the church's hymnody with practically every breath they take. I consider the persistence of hymnic memory a great blessing received from a singing church.

It is worth asking ourselves what songs are playing in our heads as we go about the day. During a recent week, I was unable to escape the voice of Allison Kraus, singing: "To Canaan's land I'm on my way, where the soul of man never dies. My darkest night will turn to day, where the soul of man never dies." For me it felt like a better soundtrack for plowing through email than, say, Madonna's "Living in a material world, and I am a material girl." Maybe the gospel song speaks to my longing to exceed the material boundaries of my life. Whatever the songs we remember, it may be that one of the greatest struggles for liberation in our postmodern media culture is the struggle over which songs will be in our heads as we live our lives and how we respond to them—as consumers or as disciples.

Praise and protest

The power of a mutually subjected community of friends that sings together is glorious and challenges the world. Anabaptist martyr Anna Janz of Rotterdam was arrested for singing an Anabaptist song in public. In a letter to her son before she was executed, she urged him to join the "poor, cast-off little flock, which is despised and rejected by the world," to "flee the shadow of this world," and to "trample under foot all unrighteousness, the world and all that is in it."[7] Anabaptists like her did not mean hostility toward the earth—God's good creation—but rather confrontation with the forces of death and darkness. These are forces that seek to divide creation, to possess it, and to use those made in the image of God as instruments in their political and ecclesiastical domination.[8] Anna Janz and her friends understood that the central strength of the little flock was doxology—praise and sacrifice to God. "Whatever you do," she admonished, "do it all to the praise of [God's] name."[9]

Anabaptists understood the power of song not just for building communities of faith, but for strengthening their resolve in the face of persecution and death. Accounts in the *Martyrs Mirror* frequently mention how they "boldly and joyfully sang" on the way to execution.[10] "I sing with exultation," wrote Felix Manz in a farewell before he was executed. It is a thought that was soon turned into a song that is still sung by Anabaptist communities today. "All my heart's delight is God who brings salvation, frees from death's dread night. I praise thee Christ of heaven, who ever shall endure, who takes away my sorrow, keeps me safe and secure."[11]

Such bold and forceful singing has been the basis for many social movements with roots in the church. Think of the unity and strength created by the gospel singing traditions during the American civil rights movement. People repeated their conviction again and again in a variety of improvised rhythms and harmonies, so that it became true in the singing and the doing: "We shall overcome some day." Likewise it is hard to imagine the South African anti-apartheid movement without the joyful and insistent freedom songs that accompanied and energized and unified their struggle. For Christians, and indeed for many communities of faith and action, changing the world means singing a liberating song.

A community that can produce and be shaped by such liberating songs is a community that is visibly different from the apparent order of things, a "remnant" community.[12] It is a community liberated from Egypt or Babylon or from whatever prevailing imperial identity rules at the time. The peace that it seeks is not the peace of accommodation or compromise with the structures and powers of the world but a reconciled way of life amidst the disorder and conflict of the age. Such a community of hope cannot be assimilated because it refuses to accept that the limits and realities of the present structures of order will have the last word. In the praise of God's name this community remembers its true home.

For reflection and discussion

1. What kinds of singing help build community? Are there forms of singing that detract from community?
2. In what ways has music shaped your self-understanding? Consider why you like the music that you do.
3. Evaluate some of the lyrics associated with current popular music. What kind of world do these songs imagine? How does this world compare with the world of the Bible?
4. Why does music provoke controversy in many church settings?
5. What knowledge have you gained from old songs that speak from a different time and place?

Chapter 12

CONFRONT THE WORLD

Because the messianic community seeks to be a confrontational community of hope, Paul argues that it must "come out from them and be separate" (2 Corinthians 6:17) from unbelievers, or "the world"—it inflects the call of Christ regarding the habits of a given social order. An early Anabaptist confession places a very clear demand on the Christendom that assimilated the church to the political order: "go out from Babylon and the earthly Egypt, that we may not be partakers in their torment and suffering."[1] This call for separation in the *Schleitheim Brotherly Union* is rooted in the biblical call that Paul was echoing from the prophets: "touch nothing unclean" (2 Corinthians 6:17). In this text, holiness is a condition for becoming the people of God: "then I will welcome you" (2 Corinthians 6:17).

Missional separation

Some people wonder if it is possible to be both separate and mission-minded. For me mission is not possible without separation. For the church and its members to actually remember the whole meaning of our mission, we need to be first called out from the world to which we minister. J. Denny Weaver describes this as a "socially active alternative community."[2]

Michael Sattler, one of the authors of the *Schleitheim Confession* demonstrated this relationship between separation and mission in his life. It was not until he separated himself from the civil religion of his time that his witness to the truth of the gospel had public and controversial visibility. For him separation clearly did not mean withdrawal but rather confrontation.

Because he challenged the integration of church and nation in early modern Europe, the religious and political authorities of his time deemed his witness both heretical and seditious. As a former Benedictine monk (and prior of a monastery), his life took a turn away from a withdrawn monasticism toward a controversial public witness—and the complexities of a world that included the delights and difficulties of marriage (by which he broke his monastic vows). He was someone for whom the call of Christ indeed meant leaving behind his former occupation, even though it was apparently religious.

When he was hauled in front of the court at Rottenburg, he was accused of a long list of doctrinal heresies and seditious actions, including having said that if the Muslim Turks invaded they should not be resisted, and that "if it were right to wage war, he would rather go to war against the Christians than against the Turks."[3] Such a statement is shocking even today; it questions allegiance to earthly powers that masquerade as "Christian" while doing violence in the name of security and virtue. Days later, after having had his tongue cut out and his body torn with red-hot tongs, Michael Sattler was burned at the stake. His wife, Margaretha, was drowned in the Neckar River the next day.

Today a small marker outside Rottenburg is inscribed with Michael Sattler's last words: "I have not been sent to defend the Word of God in court. We are sent to testify thereto."[4] These are the words of a disciple who has become subject to the Word, who has been transformed through baptism, who has offered his life in service, and who speaks with vulnerability on behalf of a remnant community—a people that refuse to be constrained by the legal and political structures that presume to organize reality.

Philosopher Slavoj Žižek emphasizes how Christian separation is a radical condition for the political remaking of the world. For him the creation of a community of genuine love requires separation. A dividing line is drawn between those who already belong comfortably to some ethnic or national or social group and those who do not. Radical Christianity is the community of those who are left out, or those who leave themselves out in the name of Jesus Christ. As Žižek puts it, "Christian universality, far from excluding some subjects, *is formulated from the position of the excluded*, of those for whom there is no specific place within the existing order [Žižek's emphasis]."[5]

The community of Christ to which we submit is a community of outsiders, a faithful remnant, who cannot be assimilated to the accepted order of things—to the empire of global American capitalism, for example, or to the rat race of corporate ladder climbing. Sooner or later, we find that when we take the side of the outsider, the outcast, and the dispossessed, we run into trouble. When we begin acting as if we are not aligned with this world's categories of inclusion and exclusion, nationality, race, gender, and sexuality, we confront those who prefer the way things are and who are prepared to privilege their comfortable attachment to familiar people over a disruptive concern for strangers.

This is the same kind of separation that divided Abraham from the tribal familiarity of his hometown of Ur. God called him to "set out, not knowing where he was going" for a "better country" and a city whose architect and builder is God (Hebrews 11:8-16). This is the separation of which Jesus spoke when he said that he came to divide parents from children, brothers from sisters and husbands from wives (Matthew 10:34-38; Luke 18:29-30). This is the separation that divided Michael and Margareta Sattler from the church of their youth and the authorities of their homeland. It is a separation of a remnant that lives in a separated community of exile, in faith and hope, rather than in certainty and security.

Precarious exile

Alain Epp Weaver notes that this separated community of exile is not in charge politically or theologically.[6] The community is not withdrawn and obsessed about its own survival;

instead, it depends on God alone for its future. This community does not seek to defend its own perspectives so much as to discover amidst the diversities of human existence witnesses to the truth of the Word of God. It is willing to be disrupted by the world beyond it, even as it bears witness to the disruption of all things by the gift of Jesus Christ.[7]

A story of martyrdom from Rwanda reminds us of the unlikely witness to unity and reconciliation that results from nonresistant separation from worldly political divisions. During the horrific season of mass slaughter involving Hutus and Tutsis in 1994, a gathering of some 13,500 Christians of various denominational stripes in the Ruhanga parish outside Kigali refused to divide into tribes, claiming they were all one in Christ. The militia responded by killing all of these Christians who refused to organize themselves according to political divisions.[8] This tragic story is also a resurrection story, for the memory of the Ruhanga martyrs continues to provide grounding for the hope of reconciliation and for a determination not to take sides in the blind divisions that persist in worldly politics.[9]

But the hope of a holy remnant community doesn't only make the unity of the dispossessed visible through dramatic martyrdom. This holy hope can guide the decisions and practices of professionals who seek to be subject to the community of Christ in their daily work. Mitch Kingsley is an attorney in the town of Bluffton, Ohio. Much of his work involves helping clients negotiate real estate transactions, plan legacies and gifts, and settle inheritances. He tells the story of a client who shared a beneficiary and trustee status for a significant legacy with a sibling. The discovery that the sibling hired an attorney nurtured the client's growing mistrust. Mitch wondered, "How will I characterize the sibling to my client and what attitudes will I encourage? Will I encourage mistrust and help tear apart the relationship even farther, so that it might never recover?"[10] In a profession where it is assumed that the ethical thing to do is "zealous representation of the client," raising such questions can be seen as not only countercultural but even risky or unethical. Mitch says that he encouraged his client to see that the relationship with a sibling had as much, if not more, value than the money involved.

Furthermore, Mitch notices how difficult it is to transcend the antagonistic stance that is so central to the legal profession. When he talks with his fellow attorneys he wonders, "Will I give the impression that I am looking for a fight or that I want to serve each of our clients by keeping the door open for future relationships?"

This attorney has learned the discipline of a community of baptism and defenselessness. The countercultural wisdom that challenges conventional legal wisdom—seeking to wipe away antagonism and division and striving to heal—is the result of Mitch's immersion in a community of faith where he makes himself accountable. His decision to pursue this profession was tested with his church. Although he was fascinated by law and concerned with the failures of justice he was not convinced that the practice of law was compatible with what he calls "the high calling placed on me by baptism."

Following a year and a half of discussions, his fellow church members sent Mitch off to law school. This being sent by the church shapes Mitch's priorities profoundly. He continues to regard it as experimental and precarious whether it is possible to be both a Christian and an attorney, but observes that "all of our careers are experimental" from the perspective of carrying out the call of Christ.

Chris Huebner describes this precariousness as a radical reformation stance that "involves a dedicated willingness to subject one's own standpoint to criticism and a corresponding attitude of vulnerable openness to new and potentially hostile voices."[11] Such a stance is crucial for life together in community, both the community of the church and the communities of civic and professional engagement in which we are also immersed. It is a faith stance in the sense that believers know that it is not up to them to "secure the truth of the Christian faith."[12] Thus, faithful believers who seek to follow Christ amidst the complexities of everyday life are open to revision and critique from others precisely because of their fidelity to a call that throws the usual order of things out of whack, that subverts complacency, and that leads to freedom.

Faithful church

It should be apparent by now that the sort of church community to which we are subject in our daily lives is not primarily a denomination or a tradition or any obviously established institution that calls itself "the church." I am advocating fidelity to what Peter Dula calls the "fugitive church," that gathering of two or three in the name of Christ where obedience to the call of Christ becomes visible—the "occasional intimacy of two or three."[13] It might be a gathering of friends that encourage one another to discover their true humanity; it might be a small group of believers at work who gather for regular Bible study and prayer, reminding one another of who they are amidst the challenges and conflicts of daily life; it might even happen in some institutional church settings.

Certainly this faithful, fugitive church was visible when Christians of all denominations in Rwanda collectively refused to organize themselves by tribes, even at the cost of their lives. But equally important, this faithful, fugitive church is made visible whenever Christians like Mitch Kingsley subject themselves to the communal disciplines of love and reconciliation in their occupational practices—even when it calls into question the "proper" way of doing things.

When the church is understood as a community of fidelity to Christ beyond any single institution, then we are no longer invested in securing any particular form of that church. The question is not whether "our" church will make it, but rather whether we will join the body of Christ that appears in our time and place. This body is separate from the worldliness of convention and empire and so-called common sense that restrains the hope and delight of living in Christ's freedom. And this body does not rely on us to make it exist. As conservative Mennonite writer Lester Bauman puts it in his book *The Little Flock*, "God will have a remnant no matter what happens. The question is not whether the church will survive but whether you and I will be part of it."[14]

The question of who *we* are lies at the center of this practice of community. How we use the plural pronoun is evidence of our allegiance. Is it *we* who elect a president, who are fighting a war on terrorism, or who win the World Series? If so, we will become overly invested in the outcomes of such elections or wars or athletic events. Is it rather *they* who are fighting the empire's wars and winning elections? Saying that it is *they* reminds us that our ultimate allegiance is not with the party or the nation or the ball team.

Who are *we*? Let it be said that we are Christ's above all else.

For reflection and discussion

1. How separate should the church be from society? Are there practices of separation that detract from the church's mission? Are there practices of assimilation that detract from the church's mission?

2. How can the bonds of church community be maintained during the week while we are at work or at home?

3. Have you experienced precarious relationships with people who do not share your Christian viewpoint? What are some ways to express the peace of Jesus Christ in the midst of such precariousness?

4. How can we express gracefully our refusal to participate in the *we* of the empire? How does such a refusal contribute to the mission of the church?

5. What are some ways that life together in the church can be a gift to be offered rather than a treasure to be protected?

WITNESS:
BECOMING PRIESTLY

Chapter 13

SACRIFICE YOURSELF

As baptized believers, fashioned into a new community, our lives are witnesses of God's reconciling work, a work that involves both sacrifice and thanksgiving. As members of the community of those who otherwise have no community (1 Peter 2:10), we are ministers of God's love, prepared to offer the grace of God to our brothers and sisters in Christ, and to all whom God seeks to save; that is, everyone. We are to become mediators of God's healing and hope; that is to say, we are to become priests.

Universal ministry

When I was sixteen years old and baptized into the Zion Conservative Mennonite Church, among the commitments I made was a willingness to serve as a minister for the congregation, should I be chosen. This question—which was asked of all male candidates for baptism in my congregation—was the most sobering of all the questions I was asked during that decisive time in my life. In my congregation ministers did not receive a salary but were expected to devote their whole life to the well-being of the congregation, even while keeping a full-time job. To be selected as a minister was a completely life-altering event. Many young men and their spouses lived in fear and dread of this calling.

The willingness to be a minister, of course, was part of a larger commitment that I made along with all the baptismal candidates of both genders to submit to the church and to accept its rule and call in my life. If the church asked me to do something on behalf of its mission, I was expected to accept.

While I never was called to be a minister, I was called to numerous other offices in the life of my childhood congregation. At one point the congregation selected me to be an usher, which meant standing at the entrance each Sunday to greet all the men with a holy kiss and helping people find seats during a crowded meeting. I was also asked to be the congregation's song leader during one of the yearly cycle of offices, which meant that I needed to lead the congregation in hymns every Sunday morning and be available on other occasions as asked. Both of these offices made me anxious and nervous. I really didn't want to kiss all the men or lead the singing, but I did these things nevertheless because when I was baptized I had promised to accept the church's call on my life.

More recently, my current congregation called me to be a deacon. One of the duties of our deacons is to serve communion and clean up afterward. The first time I did this, I found it challenging to make sure the bread and juice were properly passed from one row to another. Managing public practices gracefully is not necessarily in my skill set. Yet the patience of those I was serving helped mitigate my awkwardness, as did their helpful cues about where to go next. Although I did not feel in control I felt my church community supported me in my service.

Accepting such calls from the church is a concrete way to learn to follow after Christ in discipleship, to present our bodies as a "living sacrifice, holy and acceptable to God," and to "not be conformed to this world, but [to] be transformed by the renewing of [our] minds" so as to discern God's will—"what is good and acceptable" (Romans 12:1-2).

This call to sacrifice is probably not very attractive to twenty-first century Christians who have adopted a consumerist attitude toward the church. Michael Budde and Robert Brimlow call this attitude "Christianity, Incorporated."[1] Such a church becomes a service provider rather than a service solicitor, and customers, as we know, reserve the right to shop elsewhere if the price is too high or the service falls short.

A key feature of the service provider type of church is what some have called a "hireling ministry" that employs the "religious specialist."[2] In this model, the church hires pastors that it expects to service their needs—marry, bury, and baptize, with perhaps some free counseling thrown in along the way.

Virgil Vogt describes the two-tier system of expectation that arises with this model.[3] On the one hand we expect pastors to give their lives over to the needs of the church, to move where they are needed, and to respond to the broader church's call to denominational offices and service. On the other hand, we expect the rest of the church (what some call the laity) to make their life decisions based on pragmatic or personal criteria such as job security or climate preference. I challenge the popular conviction that paid pastors are the only people whose lives should be wholly devoted to the church.

I am convinced that all Christians, whether pastors or not, are summoned to give themselves to the mission of the church; that is, to the call to serve God and neighbor as ambassadors of Jesus Christ in every station or occupation. In joining the church, Christians are not making a consumer choice but rather responding to a demanding and liberating calling. All Christians are called to ministry. Only by giving our lives to the ministry of the church in response to this call, can believers become part of what the apostle Peter called "a holy priesthood" that offers "spiritual sacrifices acceptable to God through Jesus Christ" (1 Peter 2:5).

Peaceable sacrifice

To call for sacrifice is troublesome in our time and place. The language of sacrifice has often been used in the church and the surrounding society to deprive people of the opportunity to exercise their God-given gifts, rather than to encourage them to offer their gifts as spiritual sacrifices or to give up self-centeredness in order to reclaim the freedom of Jesus Christ.

Moreover, the language of sacrifice in our national culture is commonly used to describe the willingness of people to kill and be killed in the pursuit of war. And, indeed, soldiers do sacrifice themselves, as well as others, on behalf of the policies that are presumed to protect the nation. But the sacrifice of war, noble as it is seen to be in our society, is still a sacrifice that repeats the age-old scapegoating habits of fallen humanity: making a visible enemy the locus of the evil that threatens and then seeking to rid the world of evil by sacrificing that enemy.

In our context, that enemy may be nefarious characters like Hitler, Osama bin Laden, or all the people on death row awaiting execution. It might be the latest in a list of stereotyped and persecuted social groups that are perceived as threatening because of their difference, whether that be in religious habit, skin color, ethnic background, gendered practices, or sexual orientation. The powers of this world seek to maintain and extend their authority through such sacrifices, and say that they are in the interest of our safety and well-being. The victims of the sacrificial scapegoating practices of the powers often seek to fight back, resulting in what we call terrorism, suicide bombing, and other tactical acts of physical violence and killing. This type of response only reinforces the credibility of the sacrificial violence perpetrated by the powers. Following Rene Girard, S. Mark Heim has eloquently described this vicious cycle of sin and violence as a "no-win choice between using violence to stem violence (which is only more of the sacrificial prescription) and simply joining the line of victims."[4]

The sacrifice I am calling for is not a sacrifice that repeats or reinforces an ideology that seeks to save the self by scapegoating another. It does not give up spiritual and vocational gifts in order to avoid confrontation or risk. The sacrifice that Christians are called to offer is the sacrifice of Christ, a sacrifice that reveals to all humanity the awful cycle of sin and death to which we have been subjected and from which Christ's life, death, and resurrection frees us. This sacrifice is a living sacrifice, a celebration of the life that has been given to us through Christ's resurrection, and a refusal to protect with violence what has been given with grace.

The student who decides to prepare for a low-paying career in social work because she desires to use her gifts to serve others is making such a biblical life-giving sacrifice. The father who gives up a well-paying job in order to devote more time to his family is making such a loving sacrifice. The conscientious objector who puts down his weapons and refuses to fight, even though he risks prosecution or persecution, is offering a life-affirming sacrifice.

Jesus Christ's sacrifice of peace and of resurrection is already given to us. When we accept the calling of Christ to come and live, we receive this peaceable sacrifice, and we offer it joyfully to the world with our own lives and lips. Sacrificing ourselves is nothing less than replacing our own efforts to be good with the righteousness and goodness of Jesus Christ. So, when we decide to offer our lives to the service of Christ's body, we give up the need to justify ourselves or to be flawless in our discipleship. Instead, we offer our lives with joy and in the freedom with which Christ has made us free (Galatians 5:1).

Parents may question the virtue of investing thousands of dollars in an educational experience that prepares for a life of service rather than profit. Financial advisors may question the wisdom of giving up a job that offers presumed economic security. A nationalistic community may doubt the moral courage of a conscientious objector. Yet, we need not defend the peaceable sacrifice of Jesus Christ that we receive and offer to others; we know that our living sacrifice is pleasing to God and carries with it the power of God to truly change the world.

For reflection and discussion

1. What priestly service should the church expect of its members? Does the church typically ask too much or too little of its members today?
2. What are circumstances in which it would be wise to reject a call of the church?
3. Who are the faith heroes that have strengthened your service to God and neighbor?
4. Is the word "sacrifice" helpful in considering what kind of demand the church makes of its members? Are there better words for calling people to become mediators of God's healing and hope?
5. How can we respond to the needs of the church and the world in a way that offers the sacrifice of Jesus Christ, and not our own deeds, as the saving action we take?

Chapter 14

PRAISE GOD

When we accept the Christian calling of life together in the body of Christ, we present our bodies as "living sacrifices" (Romans 12:1). We do this first by presenting our physical bodies to our fellow believers in a gathering of praise and worship of the Creator. As Dietrich Bonhoeffer notes, "The physical presence of other Christians is a source of incomparable joy and strength to the believer."[1] This is preparation for the thankful offering of our lives as witnesses to the world—a witness that has a long history, beginning with the prophets in the Bible.

Joyful witness

Like the prophets, we have received the gift of a truth that can be seen as a burden that undermines our comfort with the ways of this world. For example, we resist conspicuous consumption. We doubt the policies of our own nation. At the same time, when we discover that our lives can make the peaceable and empowering sacrifice of Jesus Christ visible, we are able to experience profound joy and gratitude for this empowerment.

The counterintuitive joy associated with such sacrifice is nowhere more vivid than in the holy history of saints, martyrs, and dissenters who offer their lives as a witness to the renewed and reconciled way of Christ amidst the scapegoating violence

of the surrounding culture. These witnesses have aligned themselves with the cross and thus with the grain of the universe, and
are therefore empowered to stand and act in truth—exposing the
lies and blindness of our human societies. These witnesses offer
what Tripp York calls a "doxological response to the world's
rebellion against its Creator," offering their bodies as sacrifices
while refusing to sacrifice the bodies of others.[2] York shows how
the offering of bodies in spectacular witness to the power of the
resurrection is a most persuasive political witness to the triumph
of the Lamb and the hope of a new earth, a new city, as described
in the book of Revelation (Revelation 7).[3] The key dimension of
this witness is the joyful praise of God.

One such joyful witness was Lisjken Dirks. In Antwerp Lisjken and her husband, Jerome Segers, were imprisoned, severely
tortured, and executed for their faith. The *Martyrs Mirror*
account says that both "surrendered their bodies in great stead-
fastness to God as a well-pleasing sacrifice."[4] Jerome was burned
at the stake on September 2, 1551 and Lisjken, who was preg-
nant while in prison, was permitted to deliver her child before
being put alive into a sack and thrown into the Scheldt River six
months later on February 19, 1552.[5]

Lisjken and Jerome left behind a trove of letters to one
another and to their congregation where they describe their
experiences in prison and their debates with the authorities who
were threatened by their witness. The letters reveal a passionate and loving relationship between husband and wife and a
profound commitment to "following the Lamb, whithersoever
he goeth."[6] Because she read and interpreted the Bible, Lisjken
was accused of abandoning her proper station as a woman.
The authorities asked, "Why do you trouble yourself with the
Scriptures; attend to your sewing."[7] Jerome, in his return letter,
encourages her: "Although they may tell you to attend to your
sewing, this does not prevent us; for Christ has called us all,
and commanded us to search the Scriptures, since they testify
of him."[8]

At the root of their understanding of their actions was a
belief that they were taking on the worldly powers and witnessing to the God of peace. Jerome writes: "We must overcome

the world, sin, death and the devil, not with external swords or spears, but with the sword of the Spirit, which is the Word of God . . ."[9] He urges her repeatedly to "fight valiantly . . . for the glory of God."[10]

Underlying the mutual encouragement in these letters is a profound spirit of joy and praise to God. They greet one another with "grace, peace, and joy." Lisjken expresses thanks that "God the Father had showed such love to us that he gave His dear Son for us."[11]

While she was in prison Lisjken sang beautiful hymns, comforting the other prisoners. When the authorities sent some religious specialists to visit her—monks who functioned like chaplains—she refused to listen to them and sang them a song instead. When crowds gathered outside her window she addressed them with a brief sermon from her cell window and then sang until the prison guards pulled her away from the window.[12] She was executed secretly in the middle of the night.

Against the powers

The account of Lisjken Dirks, like so many other stories in the *Martyrs Mirror*, contains the crucial elements of joyful sacrifice to which all Christians are called as members of the royal priesthood. These are: being a communal witness rooted in the Word of God against the powers who seek to usurp God's role in the world, giving over of one's whole life to the struggle that ensues when the powers are challenged, and joyfully praising and worshipping God amidst the drama that unfolds.

These elements are present whenever members of Christ's body confront the forces of darkness and death. In 1920 a Goshen College student named Clayton Kratz accepted the church's call to join a growing movement to assist refugees from famine and war in Russia. Responding affirmatively to a famous telegram that asked "Can we depend on you?" Kratz traveled to the Ukraine along with two other relief workers, where he disappeared, never to be heard from again.[13] It is clear from his correspondence that he was not only dutifully answering the call of the church but delighting in the adventurous journey that included sightseeing in Greece and

Turkey. Newly discovered archival materials suggest he was executed by the Russian government on suspicion of being a spy.[14] Kratz was part of a relief project that would bear witness to God against the powers and ultimately rescue thousands of refugees in Europe during both World Wars.

In a recent book, Charles Marsh tells the story of how John Perkins also confronted the powers with his witness. Perkins became involved in the civil rights movement somewhat reluctantly, after re-encountering the social justice theology in the Bible. In 1969 he helped lead a student protest in Plain, Mississippi, demanding the inclusion of black Americans in the economic life of the town. After nineteen students were arrested and Perkins showed up at the courthouse to negotiate with the authorities, he was arrested and subjected to a night of brutality that nearly killed him. His wife, Vera Mae, and twenty friends rescued him singing "We Shall Overcome." Perkins devoted the rest of his life to building antiracist and economically interdependent communities of reconciliation. According to Marsh, "Perkins' 'three R's' (of relocation, reconciliation, and redistribution) add up to a social agenda more radical than any advanced by the civil rights movement, placing far greater demands on white financial resources and moral reserves than even the most ambitious policies circulated in the halcyon days of the Great Society."[15]

People like Kratz and Perkins responded to the call of Jesus Christ through the flawed and limited body of Christ we call the church. Today the great challenge of the church is to discover once again how to make the heroic and joyful call of Christ concrete and visible for its members so that we too can respond.

We sometimes pass over too quickly the ways in which such sacrifices of praise are already witnessing to the world. In my congregation, for example, there is a father who thankfully devotes the better part of each day to parenting his son with Down syndrome. I think of a college professor who enthusiastically travels to Colombia every spring to work for a month with Christian Peacemaker Teams. I think of the small group of prayerful protestors who gather in our town square to witness for life whenever an execution happens in our state. In all of these sacrifices, and so many more, the God of Jesus Christ, who is the God of the weak and the poor, receives public praise.

For reflection and discussion

1. What joyful sacrifices have you witnessed? What stories of sacrifice have inspired or challenged you?
2. How do stories of dramatic and costly sacrifice, such as those found in the *Martyrs Mirror*, relate to the less dramatic sacrifices we are called to make as members of the church?
3. How do our sacrifices of praise make a difference in the world?
4. What happens when sacrifice is not joyful?
5. How might we make our acts of worship and praise more publicly visible?

Chapter 15

SHOW THE WORLD

The calling of a pastor is to be for the church what the church is to be for the world. No one has more responsibility to make their priestly vocation visible than those whom Anabaptists called shepherds or servants of the Word. It is a vocation with high and joyful demands.[1] A significant feature of that pastoral calling is the call to preach—to model for the congregation how it might proclaim by its own words and deeds the wonder and mercy of God found in the Scriptures. The pastoral station is complex, shaped by the mystery, as well as the incarnation, of the Word of God. One dimension of this mystery is the pastor's modeling of both priestly and prophetic roles to the congregation.

Priest and prophet

Walter Brueggemann notes that the Old Testament presents conflicting views about priestly and prophetic roles—between a God who demands and a God who saves.[2] The priest emphasizes the purity and holiness of God's people; their difference from the society around them. The prophet calls for justice and love to prevail over all excessive concern about security and purity. For example, some Scriptures argue for withdrawing from foreigners while others urge the welcome of strangers. Some Scriptures obsess over the details of proper ritual sacrifices while others insist that God prefers obedience rather than sacrifice. The priest is concerned with the integrity of the community's witness. The prophet is concerned with the liberation from communal injustice.[3]

Brueggemann urges Christians to resist collapsing these concerns and to listen carefully to these competing scriptural testimonies as if to an unfolding argument among deeply committed partisans.[4] This unresolved tension in Scripture reveals the limits of human perception of God and prevents any one-sided view from getting out of hand.[5] The pastor's most challenging obligation is to straddle this debate and to show the congregation how to be concerned both with the church's holiness and with its mission.

My friend Daniel Hughes pastors an emerging interracial church in the nearby city of Lima called the Future Church. As someone who had been employed with the city's housing authority he knows the daily struggles many of his neighbors face in order to find shelter. He remembers the day he got a call to meet with other black pastors to discuss their response to the shooting of Tarika Wilson described in chapter 5. When he learned the details of Tarika's life she went from a story on the news to a human being who had struggled against considerable odds to overcome her surroundings: "She was poor, she had a record, and she was trying to survive; in fact, she was headed to college the very next week."[6]

For Daniel this was a call to get it right this time, to make it clear that her life mattered. For him it was a call to get close to people, particularly people who are different from oneself. So he and other community leaders have been involved with promoting a community project that brings together people with resources and those who are struggling so that they can build relationships and bridges of hope. As a pastor, Daniel is committed to the future of the church; as someone who sees the struggles and challenges of his neighbors, he is prepared to give up the comfort zone of conventional boundaries to respond: "When it comes to these issues, doctrine does not matter; when it comes to bread, we just need to get to work distributing it."[7]

Daniel's double role as a priestly leader of his congregation and a prophetic advocate for those who are left behind in his community is an example of being a shepherd. Like the shepherd in the biblical parable told by Jesus (Luke 15:4-7), Daniel both cares for his flock and also is prepared to turn his attention away from the well-being of that flock to go seek out the one lost lamb.

Congregation and proclamation

In his book *What Would Jesus Deconstruct?* John Caputo demonstrates how in this parable of the lost sheep justice exceeds the limits of law; it calls into question the adequacy of following the rules when we are seeking the kingdom of God and its righteousness. "Laws have to do with the ninety-nine, but justice has to do with the one lost sheep, with the one lost coin, with the widow, the orphan, and the stranger."[8]

The mission of the church also carries this two-fold dimension found in Scripture: both the visible institutional structure of the church and a commitment that goes beyond the institution.[9] One task of the shepherd—the pastor—is to proclaim this commitment beyond the visible church, so that the congregation can catch a glimpse of this vision and act in accordance with the renewed world that God is bringing about.

Of course, this proclamation can be either accepted or rejected. Writing about preaching, Russell Mast says: "The Christian preacher is not the successor of the Greek orator such as Cicero, but of the Hebrew prophet such as Isaiah. The orator comes with an inspiration, the prophet with a revelation."[10] It is not up to the preacher to persuade; the preacher relies on the power of God—the power of powerlessness—more than on the appeal of rhetorical tactics. "For the message about the cross is foolishness to those who are perishing, but to us who are being saved it is the power of God," Paul writes to the Corinthians (1 Corinthians 1:18).

In Anabaptist theology, such reliance on the power of God for preaching is congregation-centered, not preacher-centered. The preacher is less an orator who designs a text with intrinsic authority and more a shepherd who responds to the concerns and gifts of the congregation. Mast says that such a pastor is deeply identified with the congregation and maintains close and caring relationships with the people of the congregation. Preaching that addresses such a passionately loved audience is "dialogue and not monologue."[11] Thus, the process of discovering truth continues even during the moment of proclamation; it doesn't involve just "Jesus and you," but the community of faith gathered around the Scriptures and led by the Holy Spirit.[12] And this scene of discovery is the place where we are called to life together in Christ. We are participating in this call by responding again and again to the proclaimed and discerned Word, inviting others to respond, bearing witness to the truth of the Word made flesh—the love of Jesus Christ.

It is the task both of the pastor and of the whole priesthood—all of us who have been baptized—to bear witness to this proclaimed word, to live out in the flesh what cannot be envisioned, to be holy experiments for the kingdom of God in which Christ's life is being reproduced.[13]

Harold Bender describes the key aspects of this ministry of witness: mutual edification, proclaiming the gospel, good works, and prophecy. In other words, the people of God build one another up, they offer the good news to the world, they care for their neighbors and enemies, and they critique the world's unfaithfulness. These ministries correspond broadly with the practices I have been urging throughout this book. They are ultimately ministries of service, by which the world can experience the presence of the servant become Lord, Jesus Christ. Or, stated biblically, these ministries are the means by which Christians carry out their vocation in the great commission, to make disciples of all nations by teaching and baptizing and making the presence of Jesus Christ visible in the world, until the end of the age (Matthew 28:19-20).

It should be clear by now that this vocation is the task of all believers, the one unambiguous calling that should pervade all that we do. All of our work, all of our responsibilities, all of our life's activities must be taken up as responses to this calling. We are called to be witnesses wherever we go. As witnesses, we may be called to heroic and prophetic performances of faithfulness, as in the case of martyrs such as Anabaptist martyr Lisjken Dirks, drowned for her faith, and

Marian Fisher, the Amish girl who was willing to die for her friends. But we are also called to ordinary faithfulness, making visible on a daily basis the reconciling Lord we serve.

At times this calling will involve actually saying something about our commitment to Jesus Christ and making an invitation to join the body of Christ. Those of us who work for church-related institutions are privileged to be able to offer such verbal witness without ambiguity. As I teach and mentor students at a Mennonite university, I take every opportunity to urge them to be involved in the faith. "Go to church," I tell my students repeatedly. It is a delight to me when graduating seniors tell me that their first priority after graduation will be to connect with a community of believers that can help them make the transition to life in the world of work.

As members of Christ's body, we should not hesitate to invite others to join us in our community life. Indeed, the primary feature of our verbal witness should be an invitation to come and see, to come and live. In a time when evangelism has all too often been reduced to a verbal contract—accepting Christ as my personal Savior—our proclamation of the whole gospel should be an embracing invitation to our neighbors to be part of the same body that has given us life.

While proclamation and invitation are crucial, in many workplace contexts the more typical witness will be showing the world that we belong to Christ through our daily actions and attitudes. My wife Carrie's experience illustrates how such bodily witness can be performed. For many years, she worked at the local county board for developmental disabilities (DD), which offers services to mentally challenged and developmentally disabled people in our area. Her work as a habilitation manager involved attending to the needs of people her agency served and also supervising staff in her department.

The organization struggled with the increasingly complex and contradictory issues related to relying on government money. She confronted many obstacles to achieving the service goals of her agency: time-consuming paperwork and arbitrary classifications which distinguish who does and who doesn't get support. It was a context of declining resources, increasing

demand, and work overload, all of which strained interdepart-
mental relationships and created stress and anxiety.

Yet amidst all this dysfunction, Carrie remained committed to her own sense of mission "to serve God by serving
others." Each day she looked for opportunities to fulfill this
mission through her relationships with clients, by the way
she treated her staff, and in the mediating role she fulfilled
between administrators and staff.

The church—and the world—often overlook the profound
importance of stations that need to juggle scarce resources in
ways that offer hope and life in a world of entropy and neglect.
Indeed, even the people who work in such jobs frequently forget the significance of their work. It is the role of the church
not to forget and to help people to remember the significance
of their stations. It is the role of the church to be a kingdom of
priests who live out the kingdom of God—to be for the world
what a good pastor is for the church. Carrie and so many other
extraordinary Christians in ordinary jobs know that this is the
case, even though the church has sometimes neglected to equip
them with language and resources for their mission.

Moreover, it is often tempting with this kind of work to
eventually yield to cynicism and to adopt an ethic of survival.
Today, Carrie still works in the DD world but now as a soft-
ware specialist who provides technical support to the DD. She
changed roles in part to free herself from the demands her
earlier position made on her time and her well-being. Like
many people, she needed to make the same decision Abraham
did, whether to go or to stay—in a context, such as the highly
mobile setting of American culture, where staying can also be
the faithful and countercultural thing to do. In a way, Carrie
both went and stayed.

Carrie tells me about her everyday opportunities for faithful witness. While it may seem quite mundane, an important
dimension of her ministry of service is smiling at people, even
when she does not feel like it. "Smiling opens doors for connection with people that otherwise are not there," she says.[14]
For her, smiling arises out of her purpose and mission, not as
an expression of feeling. It is a priestly practice, an offering

to the neighbor, like so many other everyday expressions of service to others that make a difference in the world.

Jewish ethicist Emmanuel Levinas teaches us that the face is a profound crossroads of communication with the other, the neighbor.[15] Through our faces we practice regard or rejection; reception or resistance; hospitality or hostility. In a marketplace increasingly dominated by virtual worlds of mediated communication—email, texts, teleconferences, even webcams—the presence of the body in a faithful way can be a radical act.

My friend Quentin Schultze, who I cited earlier, is a professor of communication at Calvin College. Like most college professors he has an office with a computer and a desk, books and papers. But instead of spending all his time there or in the classroom, he looks for public spaces to sit down and practice a welcoming posture that invites conversation with students and colleagues. In a world where professionals are tempted to email the colleague in the room next door, rather than getting out of their seat and presenting their bodies, Quentin's practice of public bodily hospitality is a faithful witness, one that represents the body of Christ. He has even inspired an introvert like me to make more frequent visits to the offices of my colleagues.

The lives of all Christians who witness to Jesus Christ through service to others are priestly lives. Their practices may not seem particularly outstanding. In fact, bodily presence and facial hospitality are often unremarkable. But it is through practices like these that the world is being renewed and people are discovering genuine freedom in the truth. This is the mission to which all Christians are called: to become the people of God in the world, a "priestly kingdom" (Exodus 19:6; Revelation 5:10). Through such priestly care, offering to others what we have received in Jesus Christ and in the body of Christ, we offer sacrifices in all of our life stations, sharing in the service of Christ, and in the glory of God's kingdom. That is the witness to which we who have been baptized are called, life together in the body of Christ now and forever. Come and live, go to church, change the world—the call comes to us and goes out from us, in the lives and on the lips of God's people.

For reflection and discussion

1. What pastoral duties are included in the priestly role? In the prophetic role?

2. How can congregations encourage their pastors to remain committed to both priestly and prophetic roles?

3. How can the pastors or shepherds assist members of the church in performing priestly service in their life stations? Does being paid by the church help or hinder pastors in fulfilling this ministry of equipping?

4. What are some aspects of the institutional church that may need to be sacrificed in order to reach those whom God seeks to reconcile? Are some features of the institutional church so essential that they cannot be sacrificed?

5. What kinds of priestly service have you received from others, either in church or in daily life? How has that made a difference?

CONCLUSION

My children like to ask for surprises. Before we go shopping for clothes or groceries, they ask, "Can we get a surprise?" Often they will have a specific idea of what they want—Lego building blocks or a video game cartridge. On good days, these are occasions for theoretical discussions about the contradiction in their request. They want a surprise, I point out, but they have already erased the possibility of a surprise. A surprise is something unexpected. If I get them what they asked for they will be getting something that they are already expecting as a possibility. By asking for a surprise, they have already made it difficult for me to surprise them. A surprise would be for me to do something they do not expect, to perhaps give them something they have not asked for. The best way to get a real surprise, I tell my children, is to stop asking for one.

Of course I'm aware that this is not the best response I could make to my children's repeated requests for a surprise. At some point I plan to tell them that what they really want—something new—is not a bad thing to desire. The problem is not in the desire for something new, but rather in assuming that this desire can be satisfied in a retail store. I suspect that deep down they are already aware of this truth. Any brief examination of the contents of their room—including piles of abandoned toys that at one time had held the promise of erasing boredom and generating delight—would suggest that the materials of the mall do not satisfy meaningfully or reliably beyond the very short term. But I don't want them to become cynical, to give up hope that a real surprise might happen. That is why I sometimes offer them gifts they didn't request or learn to want, gifts that will delight them beyond their expectations. For example, once the family car ended up at the local movie theater for a late showing of the new Narnia film, much to the delight of my children, who didn't even know it was showing. A moment of genuine surprise like this offers a kind of foretaste of the joy that is possible for those who become attached to Jesus Christ through baptism.

The practices I have been encouraging in this book are designed precisely for this reason: to open our bodies and minds to what cannot be expected, that for which we have not planned, "a future that is not a future present," not more of the same, but something else.[1] When undertaken prayerfully, these practices seek to liberate us to receive "the event of love that was astir in Jesus," and to give our lives in service to others, when the opportunity arises.[2] With word, water, and wine, we witness to this event—the Word made flesh and dwelling among us. Our lives are no longer constrained by the fear of death; we offer our baptized bodies to the One who has called us and promises to hold us, even in death.

These practices are thus resurrection practices: open to absolute surprise. Just as we have given our lives to Christ in baptism, at the hour of our death we can with joy offer our bodies to the One who has created and redeemed us. "We will not all die, but we will all be changed, in a moment, in the twinkling of an eye, at the last trumpet" (1 Corinthians 15:51-52). By taking away the sting of death, by giving victory over death through Jesus Christ, God has "destroyed every ruler and every authority and power" (1 Corinthians 15:24-26). My friend Ray Gingerich remarked to me recently the good news of the resurrection is that "the empire will not have the last word." And since it won't have the last word, it need not rule us now. We are free to live in Christ, to love as he loved, to follow the Lamb until our bodies find rest.

I have tried to show in this book that the church as envisioned by Scripture is essential to this life of freedom in Christ. The resurrection surprises that God has in store for us exceed all of our plans and expectations, including the churchly routines to which we become accustomed. These good surprises can reach us and transform our lives because in this weak and broken body of Christ called the church, the living God has drawn near. The promise stands: where two or three gather together in the name of Jesus Christ, God shows up. As gathered and scattered believers offer their lives in practices of service, of discovering the truth, joining the church, serving bread and wine, yielding to one another, and bearing witness to God's kingdom, God acts "in, with, and under" such faithfulness to renew and reconcile all things.[3] Can there be a higher calling than a life defined by this blessed hope?

For reflection and discussion

1. What surprises have you experienced thus far in your Christian life? What have you learned from these surprises about the will and Word of God?

2. Have you answered opportunities for Christian service in your daily life? How has this changed you? Are there such opportunities for service that you have not answered? What are good reasons to say no or yes?

3. How might routines and habits endanger our ability to respond to surprising events in our lives? Can you think of ways to prepare for such surprising events?

4. In what ways does the reality of death shape the life decisions you make? How much attention should we pay to the reality of death?

5. What do you believe the resurrection of Jesus Christ means for your life and death? How does the resurrection influence the way you see the world around you?

NOTES

Introduction

1. Virgil Vogt, *The Christian Calling* (Scottdale, Pa: Herald Press, 1961), 7.

2. Tara Parker-Pope, "Are Bad Times Healthy?" *New York Times* (October 7, 2008), 1.

3. Ibid.

4. Leonard Gross, *Prayer Book for Earnest Christians*, (Scottdale, Pa: Herald Press, 1997), 15.

5. My thinking about how artful performance practices like baptism and sharing bread construe selves and make saving knowledge possible is influenced by Scott Holland's work on theological narratives and rituals. See Scott Holland, *How Do Stories Save Us? An Essay on the Question with the Theological Hermeneutics of David Tracy in View* (Louvain: Peeters, 2006), 153-78.

Chapter One

1. See early Anabaptist leader Pilgram Marpeck who writes that "the living cross and hand of Christ shows the way, does not stand immoveable in one place, never has and never will, for it is itself the way from which the truth comes and is the truth from which life comes." Walter Klaassen, Werner Packull, and John Rempel, eds., *Later Writings of Pilgram Marpeck and His Circle*, vol. 1, *Anabaptist Texts in Translation* (Kitchener, Ont: Pandora Press, 1999), 29.

2. Thielemann van Braght, *Martyrs Mirror* (Scottdale, Pa: Herald Press, 1985), 454.

3. Dietrich Bonhoeffer, *Discipleship* (Minneapolis, Minn: Fortress Press, 2003), 81.

4. Ibid., 82. In his book on Christian community, Bonhoeffer emphasized that such a community is a gift that is made possible only through Jesus Christ: "We belong to one another only through and in Jesus Christ." Dietrich Bonhoeffer, *Life Together* (New York, NY: Harper and Row, 1954), 21.

5. Thomas Merton, *The New Man* (New York, NY: Farrar, Straus and Cudahy, 1961), 9.

6. Waldemar Janzen, *Exodus. Believers Church Bible Commentary* (Scottdale, Pa: Herald Press, 2000), 368.

7. "The Church's One Foundation," *Hymnal: A Worship Book* (Elgin, Ill; Newton, Kan; Scottdale, Pa: Brethren Press; Faith and Life Press; Mennonite Publishing House, 1992), 311.

8. Thomas Dunn, "Why I Bother," *The Mennonite* (October 1, 2010), 58.

9. Gerald J. Mast, "Bearing the Cross as a Way of Knowing," *The Cresset* (September 2010), 6-13.

10. Kareen Fehderau, "Embedded Values," *The Marketplace* (September-October 2008), 6-7.

11. According to a recent Pew survey, 71% of those surveyed are absolutely certain of their belief in God, and another 17% are fairly certain of their belief. In other words, 88% of those surveyed exhibit belief in God. However, in the same survey, only 14% of those surveyed report going to church more than once a week while 24% report going to church at least once a week. In other words, only about 40% of those surveyed go to church regularly. See the U.S. Religious Landscape Survey by the Pew Forum on Religion and Public Life: http://religions.pewforum.org/comparisons#, accessed August 29, 2008.

12. William Klassen and Walter Klaassen, eds., and trans., *The Writings of Pilgram Marpeck* (Scottdale, Pa: Herald Press, 1978), 201.

13. John Howard Yoder states this point succinctly: "The church precedes the world epistemologically. We know more fully from Jesus Christ and the context of the confessed faith than we know in other ways." John Howard Yoder, *The Priestly Kingdom* (Notre Dame, Ind: University of Notre Dame Press, 1984), 11.

14. Paul V. Stutzman, *Hiking Through: Finding Peace and Freedom on the Appalachian Trail* (Austin, Tex: Synergy Books, 2009), 193-95.

15. Ibid., 201, 229-30.

Chapter Two

1. Karl Barth, *Church Dogmatics 1.2* (Edinburgh: T&T Clark, 1956), 475.

2. "The Word of God is solid ground," *Hymnal: A Worship Book*, (Elgin, Ill; Newton, Kan; Scottdale, Pa: Brethren Press; Faith and Life Press; Mennonite Publishing House, 1992), 314.

3. A reading plan that has been helpful for me is by J. Delbert Erb, *God's Plan for the Nations: A Bible Reading Plan* (Scottdale, PA: Herald Press, 1997).

4. Walt Whitman used the phrase in his poem "Song of Myself" to refer to the narrator of his poem: "Do I contradict myself? /Very well then, I contradict myself (I am large, I contain multitudes.)" Walt Whitman, *Leaves of Grass* (New York, NY: Modern Library, n.d.), 73; Walter Brueggemann, *Theology of the Old Testament: Testimony, Dispute, Advocacy* (Minneapolis, Minn: Fortress Press, 1997), 73.

5. Clarence Bauman, ed. and trans., *The Spiritual Legacy of Hans Denck* (Leiden: E. J. Brill, 1991), 162-77.

6. Wayne Pipkin and John Howard Yoder, trans. and ed., *Balthasar Hubmaier, Theologian of Anabaptism* (Scottdale, Pa: Herald Press, 1989), 428.

7. For an excellent discussion of how diversity in the Bible and in our world serves the knowledge of the Scriptures, see Timothy J. Geddert, *All Right Now: Finding Consensus on Ethical Questions* (Scottdale, Pa: Herald Press, 2008), 28.

8. C. Arnold Snyder, *Following in the Footsteps of Christ* (Maryknoll, NY: Orbis Books, 2004), 116.

9. Bauman, *The Spiritual Legacy of Hans Denck*, 113.

10. Sara Wenger Shenk, *Anabaptist Ways of Knowing* (Telford, Pa: Cascadia Publishing House, 2003), 51.

Chapter Three

1. "The point that apocalyptic makes is not only that people who wear crowns and who claim to foster justice by the swords are not as strong as they think—true as that is: we still sing, 'O Where are Kings and Empires now of old that came and went?' It is that people who bear crosses are working with the grain of the universe." John Howard Yoder, "Armaments and Eschatology" *Studies in Christian Ethics 1*(1988), 58. Yoder's point here is that in biblical stories about coming disasters, faithful and loving

yieldedness is the only life-giving way through the shadow of death that lurks on every human and cosmic horizon. Trying to protect ourselves by stockpiling weapons and wielding political power is a strategy of living that has no long-term future.

2. Klassen and Klaassen, *The Writings of Pilgram Marpeck*, (Scottdale, Pa: Herald Press, 1978), 56.

3. Hans Hut, "On the Mystery of Baptism," in Daniel Liechty, trans. and ed., *Early Anabaptist Spirituality: Selected Writings* (New York, NY: Paulist Press, 1994), 71.

4. For an essay that explores "the gospel of all creatures" in Anabaptist writings and to understand how Christians are to read creation as God's body see Trevor Bechtel, "The Gift of Creation and Interpretation," in Alain Epp Weaver and Gerald J. Mast, *The Work of Jesus Christ in Anabaptist Perspective* (Telford, Pa: Cascadia Publishing House, 2008), 361-68.

5. These examples are from a book of essays by Bluffton University faculty that explores how a nonviolent worldview reconstitutes knowledge across the liberal arts curriculum. See J. Denny Weaver and Gerald Biesecker-Mast, *Teaching Peace: Nonviolence and the Liberal Arts* (Lanham, Md: Rowman and Littlefield, 2003).

6. Jacques Derrida, *Memoirs of the Blind* (Chicago, Ill: University of Chicago Press, 1993), 20.

7. Tobit is a character in the Old Testament apocryphal book called "Tobit." Although evangelical Protestant Christians do not regard this book as canonical, it is considered "deuterocanonical" by Catholic and Orthodox Christians. In the Anabaptist-Mennonite tradition, Tobit and other apocryphal books were highly regarded and often quoted alongside canonical Scripture. The story of Tobit is recalled and repeated at every Amish wedding, even today. Readers who wish to review the story of Tobit will need to find a Bible that includes the Old Testament apocrypha.

8. Interview with Scott Schomberg, Bluffton, Ohio, October 8, 2008.

9. Quentin Schultze, *Here I Am: Now What on Earth Should I Be Doing* (Grand Rapids, Mich: Baker Books, 2005), 15.

10. "Some Stories from Soldiers who became Conscientious Objectors," *MCC Peace Office Newsletter* (January-March 2008), 8.

11. Ibid., 9.

12. Karl Barth, *The Word of God and the Word of Man* (Boston: The Pilgrim Press, 1928), 212.

Chapter Four

1. David Morrow, "When God Keeps Sending the Enemy to Your House," *Gospel Herald*, January 13 1998, 1-3.

Chapter Five

1. Henry Funk, *A Mirror of Baptism, with the Spirit, with Water, and with Blood* (Mountain Valley, Va: Joseph Funk and Sons, 1851), 72-73.

2. Menno Simons, *The Complete Writings of Menno Simons*, trans. Leonard Verduin (Scottdale, Pa: Herald Press, 1956; reprint, 1978), 684-85.

3. Thomas F. Reynolds, *Vulnerable Communion: A Theology of Disability and Hospitality* (Grand Rapids, Mich.: Brazos Press, 2008), 42.

4. Ibid., 43.

5. William H. Willimon, "Repent," in *Bread and Wine: Readings for Lent and Easter* (Maryknoll, NY: Orbis Books, 2005), 10.

6. John Howard Yoder, *Body Politics: Five Practices of the Christian Community before the Watching World* (Scottdale, Pa: Herald Press, 2001), 30.

7. David Morrow, "When God Keeps Sending the Enemy to Your House," *Gospel Herald*, January 13 1998, 1-3.

8. Yoder, *Body Politics*, 34-35.

9. For a persuasive account of the biblical roots of human rights talk, see Christopher Marshall, *Crowned With Glory and Honor: Human Rights in the Biblical Tradition* (Telford, Pa: Pandora Press USA, 2001).

10. For a critique of rights talk from the perspective of gospel gentleness, see Stanley Hauerwas and Jean Vanier, *Living Gently in a Violent World* (Downers Grove, Ill: Intervarsity Press, 2008), 77-99.

11. Slavoj Žižek, *The Fragile Absolute* (London: Verso, 2000), 150.

12. Ibid, 129-30. For a more detailed appropriation of Žižek to a radical Christian posture, see Gerald J. Biesecker-Mast, "Deconstruction, Messianic Hope, and Just Action," in David L. Weaver-Zercher and William H. Willimon, eds., *Vital Christianity: Spirituality, Justice, and Christian Practice* (New York, NY: T&T Clark, 2005), 126-38.

13. Greg Sowinski, "Chavalia Claims Self-Defense," *The Lima News* (Friday, August 1, 2008), A7.

14. For an insightful discussion about how the rights to protection and possession are construed as natural—and therefore as the basis for investing absolute power in such an entity as the state—in the political philosophies of such influential modern thinkers as Thomas Hobbes and John Locke, see Harry Huebner, "The Nation: Beyond Secular Politics," in Jeremy Bergen, Paul G. Doerksen, and Karl Koop, eds., *Creed and Conscience: Essays in Honor of A. James Reimer* (Kitchener, Ont: Pandora Press, 2007), 257-270. Huebner proposes that the people of God brought about by the work of Jesus Christ is an alternative reconciling political body that replaces fear of the neighbor with fear of "destruction from the powers that seek to destroy what God has given us in Jesus Christ" (278).

15. See the 1527 *Schleitheim Brotherly Union* for the distinction between God's order and Christ's perfection held by early Anabaptists. John Howard Yoder, ed., *The Legacy of Michael Sattler* (Scottdale, Pa: Herald Press, 1973), 39.

16. The best account, in my view, is by John L. Ruth, *Forgiveness: A Legacy of the West Nickel Mines Amish School* (Scottdale, Pa; Herald Press, 2007).

17. Eugene Peterson, *The Jesus Way* (Grand Rapids, Mich: Eerdmans, 2006), 184.

Chapter Six

1. Cornelius Dyck, William E. Keeney, and Alvin J. Beachy, trans. and eds., *The Writings of Dirk Philips, 1504-1568* (Scottdale, Pa: Herald Press, 1992), 91-92.

2. *Ausbund Das Ist: Ethliche Schöne Christliche Lieder*, (Lancaster, Pa: Amischen Gemeinden, 1992), 490-91; Robert Riall, trans. and Galen Peters, ed., *The Earliest Hymns of the Ausbund*, vol. 3, *Anabaptist Texts in Translation* (Kitchener, Ont: Pandora Press, 2003), 126.

3. *The Interpreter's Bible*, vol. 12 (Nashville, Tenn: Abingdon Press, 1957), 238.

4. Ken Jennings and John Stahl-Wert, *The Serving Leader* (San Francisco, Calif: Berrett-Koehler Publishers, 2003), 102.

5. Nancey Murphy, *Reconciling Theology and Science: A Radical Reformation Perspective* (Waterloo, Ont: Pandora Press, 1997), 70.

6. Daniel Liechty, ed. and trans. *Early Anabaptist Spirituality: Selected Writings* (New York: Paulist Press, 1994), 73.

7. Ibid., 74.

8. Ibid., 75.

Chapter Seven

1. Rhodes has written a fine memoir about his family's experience with the Hutterites. Robert Rhodes, *Nightwatch: An Inquiry Into Solitude* (Intercourse, Pa: Good Books, 2009).

2. *The New Interpreter's Bible*, vol. 10 (Nashville, Tenn: Abingdon Press, 2002), 100.

3. Ibid., 96.

4. John J. Friesen, ed., *Peter Riedemann's Hutterite Confession of Faith*, vol. 9, *Classics of the Radical Reformation* (Scottdale, Pa: Herald Press, 1999), 119.

5. Ibid., 120.

6. Ibid., 120-21.

7. Ibid., 121.

8. Milo Kauffman, *The Challenge of Christian Stewardship* (Scottdale, Pa: Herald Press, 1955), 3.

9. Tanner effectively unmasks how capitalism holds private property to be natural and calls for an alternative economic imagination based in the grace of the gospel. Kathryn Tanner, *Economy of Grace* (Minneapolis, Minn: Fortress Press, 2005), 63.

10. Terry Falla and Beryl Turner, excerpted in Arlene Mark, ed., *Words for Worship* (Scottdale, Pa: Herald Press, 1996), no. 217.

Chapter Eight

1. John Howard Yoder, *Body Politics: Five Practices of the Christian Community before the Watching World* (Scottdale, Pa: Herald Press, 2001), 18.

2. Ibid., 20.

3. Edward Hyams, quoted in Robert C. Fuller, *Religion and Wine* (Knoxville, Tenn: University of Tennessee Press, 1996), 3.

4. William Klassen and Walter Klaassen, trans. and eds., *The Writings of Pilgram Marpeck* (Scottdale, Pa: Herald Press, 1978), 74.

5. Mark Thiessen Nation, "Washing Feet: Preparation for Service," in Stanley Hauerwas and Samuel Wells, eds., *The Blackwell*

Companion to Christian Ethics (Malden, Mass: Blackwell Publishing, 2006), 450.

6. D. Stephen Long and Tripp York, "Remembering: Offering Our Gifts," in Stanley Hauerwas and Samuel Wells, eds., *The Blackwell Companion to Christian Ethics* (Malden, Mass: Blackwell Publishing, 2006), 261.

Chapter Nine

1. John Howard Yoder, *Body Politics: Five Practices of the Christian Community before the Watching World* (Scottdale, Pa: Herald Press, 2001), 21.

2. John Longhurst, "MEDA helps restore derelict church," *The Mennonite* (May 4, 2004), 24. Some of the details of this section came from a visit to Pittsburgh and a personal interview with Jessica King in Fall of 2005. See also the Union Project website: http://www.unionproject.org/ (accessed September 20, 2011).

3. DeVonna R. Allison, "Trading House for RV, Couple Follow God's Lead," *Mennonite Weekly Review* (October 11, 2010), 3.

4. Lynn Miller, *The Power of Enough* (Goshen, Ind: MMA Stewardship Solutions, 2007), 47-57.

5. Ibid., 59-92.

6. John Howard Yoder, *The Politics of Jesus* (Grand Rapids, Mich: Eerdmans, 1994), 172.

Chapter Ten

1. William Cavanaugh, *Being Consumed: Economics and Christian Desire* (Grand Rapids, Mich: Eerdmans: 2008), 17-19.

2. Nicholas Carr, *The Shallows: What the Internet is Doing to Our Brains* (New York, NY: WW Norton, 2010), 115-43.

3. Thomas R. Yoder Neufeld, *Ephesians. Believers Church Bible Commentary* (Scottdale, Pa: Herald Press, 2002), 37.

4. David Matzko McCarthy, *The Good Life: Genuine Christianity for the Middle Class* (Grand Rapids, MI: Brazos Press, 2004), 31.

5. Ibid., 35.

6. David Kline, *Scratching the Woodchuck: Nature on an Amish Farm* (Athens, Ga: University of Georgia Press, 1997), 195-96.

Chapter Eleven

1. David F. Ford, *Self and Salvation* (Cambridge: Cambridge University Press, 1999; reprint, 2003), 122.

2. Marlene Kropf and Kenneth Nafziger, *Singing: A Mennonite Voice* (Scottdale, Pa: Herald Press, 2001), 49.

3. Ibid., 123.

4. Ibid., 51.

5. Rowan Williams, *Why Study the Past? The Quest for the Historical Church* (Grand Rapids, Mich: William B. Eerdmans Publishing Company, 2005), 92-93.

6. Ibid., 110.

7. Thieleman J. van Braght, *Martyrs Mirror* (Scottdale, Pa: Herald Press, 1985), 454.

8. John Howard Yoder clarifies the meaning of *world* in the biblical parlance: "'World' (*aion houtos* in Paul, *kosmos* in John) signifies in this connection not creation or nature or the universe but rather the fallen form of the same, no longer conformed to the creative intent." John Howard Yoder, *The Royal Priesthood* (Grand Rapids, Mich: Eerdmans, 1994), 55.

9. Thieleman J. van Braght, *Martyrs Mirror* , 454.

10. Ibid.

11. "I sing with exultation," *Hymnal: A Worship Book*, (Elgin, Ill; Newton, Kan; Scottdale, Pa: Brethren Press; Faith and Life Press; Mennonite Publishing House, 1992), 438.

12. Giorgio Agamben, *The Time that Remains* (Stanford, Ca: Stanford University Press, 2005), 57.

Chapter Twelve

1. John Howard Yoder, *The Legacy of Michael Sattler* (Scottdale, Pa: Herald Press, 1973), 38.

2. Weaver posits the socially active alternative community as a third way beyond identification with the world or withdrawal from the world. See J. Denny Weaver, "The Socially Active Community: An Alternative Ecclesiology," in Rodney Sawatsky and Scott Holland, eds., *The Limits of Perfection: A Conversation with J. Lawrence Burkholder* (Waterloo, Ont: Conrad Grebel College, 1993), 90-94.

3. John Howard Yoder, *The Legacy of Michael Sattler*, 71.

4. Ibid., 74. The story of Michael Sattler, the record of his trial, and his letter to the congregation at Horb can also be found in the *Martyrs Mirror*, 416-20.

5. Slavoj Žižek, *The Parallax View* (Cambridge, Mass: MIT Press, 2006), 35.

6. Alain Epp Weaver, *States of Exile* (Scottdale, Pa: Herald Press, 2008), 108.

7. Ibid., 97.

8. Edwina Thomas, "Can These Bones Live," *SOMA (Sharing of Ministries Abroad) Newsletter* (October 15, 1996), 11.

9. Ibid.

10. Interview with Mitch Kingsley, Bluffton, Ohio, January 18, 2007.

11. Chris Huebner, *A Precarious Peace* (Scottdale, Pa: Herald Press, 2006), 109.

12. Ibid.

13. Cited in Isaac Villegas, "A Fugitive Church," *The Mennonite* (October 16, 2008), 2.

14. Lester Bauman, *The Little Flock* (Crockett, Ky: Rod and Staff Publishers, 1999), 109.

Chapter Thirteen

1. Michael L. Budde and Robert W. Brimlow, *Christianity Incorporated: How Big Business Is Buying the Church* (Grand Rapids, Mich: Brazos Press, 2002), 83-108.

2. John Howard Yoder, *The Fullness of Christ: Paul's Revolutionary Vision of Universal Ministry* (Elgin, Ill: Brethren Press, 1987), 1-8.

3. Virgil Vogt, *The Christian Calling* (Scottdale, Pa: Mennonite Publishing House, 1961), 1-5.

4. S. Mark Heim, "No More Scapegoats: How Jesus Put an End to Sacrifice," *The Christian Century* (September 5, 2006), 23.

Chapter Fourteen

1. Dietrich Bonhoeffer, *Life Together* (New York, NY: Harper and Row, 1954), 19.

2. Tripp York, *The Purple Crown* (Scottdale, Pa: Herald Press, 2007), 23.

3. Ibid., 53-58.

4. Thieleman J. van Braght, *Martyrs Mirror* (Scottdale, Pa: Herald Press, 1985), 504.

5. N. van der Zijpp, "Lysken Dirks," in *Mennonite Encyclopedia 3*, ed. Cornelius Krahn (Scottdale, Pa: Herald Press, 1957), 427.

6. Braght, *Martyrs Mirror*, 513.

7. Ibid., 515.

8. Ibid., 516.

9. Ibid., 505.

10. Ibid., 521.

11. Ibid., 515

12. Ibid.

13. Geraldine Gross Harder, *When Apples Are Ripe: The Story of Clayton Kratz* (Scottdale, Pa: Herald Press, 1971).

14. Sidney King, "In the Footsteps of Clayton Kratz," in *Gathering at the Hearth: Stories Mennonites Tell*, ed. John E. Sharp (Scottdale, Pa: Herald Press, 2001), 212-13.

15. Charles Marsh, *The Beloved Community: How Faith Shapes Social Justice, from the Civil Rights Movement to Today* (New York, NY: Basic Books, 2005), 176.

Chapter Fifteen

1. See article five of the *Schleitheim Brotherly Union* for an early Anabaptist account of the office of the "shepherd." John Howard Yoder, *The Legacy of Michael Sattler* (Scottdale, Pa: Herald Press, 1973), 38-39.

2. Walter Brueggemann, *Theology of the Old Testament* (Minneapolis, Minn: Fortress Press, 1997), 723.

3. Ibid., 187-95.

4. Many early Anabaptists also advocated such an approach to Scripture. See, for example, Hans Denck's list of contradictory scriptural claims, a list that exemplifies the two trajectories Brueggemann describes. Clarence Bauman, trans. and ed., *The Spiritual Legacy of Hans Denck* (Leiden: E. J. Brill, 1991), 160-77.

5. Karl Barth, *Church Dogmatics 1.1* (Edinburgh: T&T Clark, 1936), 59.

6. Daniel Hughes presentation, Bluffton University Forum, Founders Hall, November 11, 2008.

7. Ibid.

8. John D. Caputo, *What Would Jesus Deconstruct?* (Grand Rapids, Mich: Baker Academic, 2007), 65.

9. Karl Barth, *Church Dogmatics 1.1*, 59.

10. Russell Mast, *Preach the Word* (Newton, Kan: Faith and Life Press, 1968), 22.

11. Ibid., 58.

12. David Greiser describes Anabaptist preaching as being done in a "communal voice," noting the practice of *Zeugniss*, or congregational response to the sermon that often occurs in Mennonite churches. See David B. Greiser and Michael A. King, eds., *Anabaptist Preaching: A Conversation Between Pulpit, Pew, and Bible* (Telford, Pa: Cascadia Publishing House, 2003), 24.

13. Harold Bender, *These Are My People: The New Testament Church* (Scottdale, Pa: Herald Press, 1962), 92.

14. Interview with Carrie Kruse, Ada, Ohio, January 23, 2007.

15. Emmanuel Levinas, *Totality and Infinity* (Pittsburgh, Pa: Duquesne University Press, 1969), 197-201.

Conclusion

1. John Caputo, *The Prayers and Tears of Jacques Derrida* (Bloomington, Ind: Indiana University Press, 1997), 77.

2. John Caputo, *What Would Jesus Deconstruct?* (Grand Rapids: Mich: Baker Academic, 2007), 112.

3. John Howard Yoder, *Body Politics: Five Practices of the Christian Community before the Watching World* (Scottdale, Herald Press, 2001), 1.

BIBLIOGRAPHY

Agamben, Giorgio, *The Time That Remains*. Stanford, Calif: Stanford University Press, 2005.

Allson, DeVonna R., "Trading House for RV, Couple Follow God's Lead." *Mennonite Weekly Review* (October 11, 2010): 3.

Ausbund Das Ist: Etliche Schöne Christliche Lieder. Lancaster, Pa: Amischen Gemeinden, 1992.

Barth, Karl. *Church Dogmatics: 1, 2, 3*. Edinburgh: T&T Clark, 1936-61.

Barth, Karl. *The Word of God and the Word of Man*. Boston: The Pilgrim Press, 1928.

Bauman, Clarence. trans., *The Spiritual Legacy of Hans Denck*. Leiden: E.J. Brill, 1991.

Bauman, Lester. *The Little Flock*. Crockett, Ky: Rod and Staff Publishers, 1999.

Bechtel, Trevor. "The Gift of Creation and Interpretation," in *The Work of Jesus Christ in Anabaptist Perspective*, edited by Alain Epp Weaver and Gerald J. Mast, 345-70. Telford, Pa: Cascadia Publishing House, 2008.

Bender, Harold. *These Are My People: The New Testament Church*. Scottdale, Pa: Herald Press, 1962.

Biesecker-Mast, Gerald J. "Deconstruction, Messianic Hope, and Just Action," in *Vital Christianity: Spirituality, Justice, and Christian Practice*, edited by David L. Weaver-Zercher and William H. Willimon, 126-38. New York, NY: T&T Clark, 2005.

Bonhoeffer, Dietrich. *Discipleship*. Minneapolis, Minn: Fortress Press, 2003.

Bonhoeffer, Dietrich. *Life Together*. New York: Harper and Row, 1954.

Braght, Thieleman J. van, *The Bloody Theater Or Martyrs Mirror of the Defenseless Christians Who Baptized Only Upon Confession of Faith and Who Suffered and Died for the Testimony of Jesus, Their Saviour, from the Time of Christ to the Year A. D. 1660*, 14th ed. Scottdale, Pa: Herald Press, 1985.

Brueggemann, Walter. *Theology of the Old Testament: Testimony, Dispute, Advocacy*. Minneapolis, Minn: Fortress Press, 1997.

Budde, Michael L. and Robert W. Brimlow, *Christianity Incorporated: How Big Business Is Buying the Church*. Grand Rapids, Mich: Brazos Press, 2002.

Caputo, John D. *The Prayers and Tears of Jacques Derrida*. Bloomington, Ind: Indiana University Press, 1997.

Caputo, John D. *What Would Jesus Deconstruct*. Grand Rapids, Mich: Baker Academic, 2007.

Carr, Nicholas. *The Shallows: What the Internet is Doing to Our Brains*. New York, NY: WW Norton, 2010.

Cavanaugh, William. *Being Consumed: Economics and Christian Desire*. Grand Rapids, Mich: Eerdmans, 2008.

Derrida, Jacques. *Memoirs of the Blind*. Chicago: University of Chicago Press, 1993.

Dunn, Thomas. "Why I Bother." *The Mennonite* (October 1, 2010): 58.

Erb, J. Delbert. *God's Plan for the Nations*. Scottdale, Pa: Herald Press, 1997.

Fehderau, Kareen. "Embedded Values." *The Marketplace* (September/October 2008): 6-7.

Ford, David F. *Self and Salvation*. Cambridge: Cambridge University Press, 1999; reprint, 2003.

Friesen, John J., ed., *Peter Riedemann's Hutterite Confession of Faith*. Scottdale, Pa: Herald Press, 1999.

Fuller, Robert C. *Religion and Wine*. Knoxville, Tenn: University of Tennessee Press, 1996.

Funk, Henry. *A Mirror of Baptism, with the Spirit, with Water, and with Blood*. Mountain Valley, Va: Joseph Funk and Sons, 1851.

Geddert, Timothy. *All Right Now: Finding Consensus on Ethical Questions*. Scottdale, Pa: Herald Press, 2008.

Greiser, David B. and Michael A. King, eds., *Anabaptist Preaching: A Conversation Between Pulpit, Pew, and Bible*. Telford, Pa: Cascadia Publishing House, 2003.

Gross, Leonard, ed. and trans., *Prayer Book for Earnest Christians*. Scottdale, Pa: Herald Press, 1997.

Harder, Geraldine Gross. *When Apples Are Ripe: The Story of Clayton Kratz*. Scottdale, Pa: Herald Press, 1971.

Hauerwas, Stanley and Jean Vanier, *Living Gently in a Violent World*. Downers Grove, Ill: Intervarsity Press, 2008.

Heim, S. Mark. "No More Scapegoats: How Jesus Put an End to Sacrifice," *The Christian Century* (September 5, 2006): 22-29.

Holland, Scott. *How Do Stories Save Us? An Essay on the Question with the Theological Hermeneutics of David Tracy in View*. Louvain: Peeters, 2006.

Huebner, Chris. *A Precarious Peace*. Scottdale, Pa: Herald Press, 2006.

Huebner, Harry. "The Nation: Beyond Secular Politics," in *Creed and Conscience: Essays in Honor of A. James Reimer*, edited by Jeremy Bergen, Paul G. Doerksen, and Karl Koop, 257-70. Kitchener, Ont: Pandora Press, 2007.

Hut, Hans. "On the Mystery of Baptism," in *Early Anabaptist Spirituality: Selected Writings*, translated and edited by Daniel Liechty, 64-81. New York, NY: Paulist Press, 1994.

Hymnal: A Worship Book. Elgin, Ill; Newton, Kan; Scottdale, Pa: Brethren Press; Faith and Life Press; Mennonite Publishing House, 1992.

The Interpreter's Bible, vol. 12. Nashville, Tenn: Abingdon Press, 1957.

Janzen, Waldemar. *Exodus. Believers Church Bible Commentary*. Scottdale, Pa: Herald Press, 2000.

Jennings, Ken and John Stahl-Wert, *The Serving Leader*. San Francisco, Calif: Berrett-Koehler Publishers, 2003.

Kauffman, Milo. *The Challenge of Christian Stewardship.* Scottdale, Pa: Herald Press, 1955.

King, Sidney. "In the Footsteps of Clayton Kratz," in *Gathering at the Hearth: Stories Mennonites Tell,* edited by John E. Sharp, 207-15. Scottdale, Pa: Herald Press, 2001.

Klaassen, Walter, Werner Packull, and John Rempel, eds. *Later Writings of Pilgram Marpeck and His Circle.* Kitchener, ON: Pandora Press, 1999.

Klassen, William and Walter Klaassen, eds., and trans., *The Writings of Pilgram Marpeck.* Scottdale, Pa: Herald Press, 1978.

Kline, David. *Scratching the Woodchuck: Nature on an Amish Farm.* Athens, Ga: University of Georgia Press, 1997.

Kropf, Marlene and Kenneth Nafziger. *Singing: A Mennonite Voice.* Scottdale, Pa: Herald Press, 2001.

Levinas, Emmanuel. *Totality and Infinity.* Pittsburgh, Pa: Duquesne University Press, 1969.

Long, D. Stephen and Tripp York, "Remembering: Offering Our Gifts," in *The Blackwell Companion to Christian Ethics,* edited by Stanley Hauerwas and Samuel Wells, 332-45. Malden, Mass: Blackwell Publishing, 2006.

Longhurst, John. "MEDA helps restore derelict church," *The Mennonite* (May 4, 2004): 24.

Mark, Arlene. ed., *Words for Worship.* Scottdale, Pa: Herald Press, 1996.

Marsh, Charles. *The Beloved Community: How Faith Shapes Social Justice, from the Civil Rights Movement to Today.* New York: Basic Books, 2005.

Marshall, Christopher. *Crowned With Glory and Honor: Human Rights in the Biblical Tradition.* Telford, Pa: Pandora Press U.S., 2001.

Mast, Gerald J. "Bearing the Cross as a Way of Knowing." *The Cresset,* September 2010, 6-13.

Mast, Russell. *Preach the Word.* Newton, Kan: Faith and Life Press, 1968.

McCarthy, David Matzko. *The Good Life: Genuine Christianity for the Middle Class.* Grand Rapids, MI: Brazos Press, 2004.

Mead, George Herbert. *Mind, Self, and Society*. Chicago, Ill: University of Chicago Press, 1935.

Merton, Thomas. *The New Man*. New York, NY: Farrar, Straus and Cudahy, 1961.

Meyendorff, Paul. "The Priesthood of the Laity," in *Christ at Work: Orthodox Perspectives on Vocation*, edited by Ann Mitsakos Bezzerides, 209-27. Brookline, Mass: Holy Orthodox Cross Press, 2006.

Miller, Lynn. *The Power of Enough*. Goshen, Ind: MMA Stewardship Solutions, 2007.

Morrow, David. "When God Keeps Sending the Enemy to Your House," *Gospel Herald* (January 3, 1998): 1-3.

Murphy, Nancey. *Reconciling Theology and Science: A Radical Reformation Perspective*. Waterloo, Ont: Pandora Press, 1997.

Nation, Mark Thiessen. "Washing Feet: Preparation for Service," in *The Blackwell Companion to Christian Ethics*, edited by Stanley Hauerwas and Samuel Wells, 441-51. Malden, MA: Blackwell Publishing, 2006.

Neufeld, Thomas R. Yoder. *Ephesians. Believers Church Bible Commentary*. Scottdale, Pa: Herald Press, 2002.

The New Interpreter's Bible, vol. 10. Nashville: Abingdon Press, 2002.

Parker-Pope, Tara. "Are Bad Times Healthy?" *New York Times* (October 7, 2008): 1.

Peterson, Eugene. *The Jesus Way*. Grand Rapids, Mich: Eerdmans.

Pipkin, Wayne, and John Howard Yoder, trans. and eds., *Balthasar Hubmaier, Theologian of Anabaptism*. Scottdale, Pa: Herald Press, 1989.

Religious Landscape Survey by the Pew Forum on Religion and Public Life: http://religions.pewforum.org/comparisons#, accessed August 29, 2008.

Reynolds, Thomas F. *Vulnerable Communion: A Theology of Disability and Hospitality*. Grand Rapids, Mich: Brazos Press, 2008.

Rhodes, Robert. *Nightwatch: An Inquiry Into Solitude*. Intercourse, Pa: Good Books, 2009.

Riall, Robert, trans. and Galen Peters, ed., *The Earliest Hymns of the Ausbund*, Kitchener, Ont.: Pandora Press, 2003.

Riedemann, Peter. *Love Is Like a Fire*. Farmington, Pa: Plough Publishing, 1993.

Riedemann, Peter. *Peter Riedemann's Hutterite Confession of Faith*, trans. John J. Friesen, Scottdale, Pa: Herald Press, 1999.

Ruth, John L. *Forgiveness: A Legacy of the West Nickel Mines Amish School*. Scottdale, Pa: Herald Press, 2007.

Schaff, Philip, ed., *The Evangelical Protestant Creeds*, Sixth ed. (The Creeds of Christendom) Grand Rapids, Mich: Baker Books, 1983; reprint, 1998.

Schlabach, Gerald. "Breaking Bread: Peace and War," in *The Blackwell Companion to Christian Ethics*, edited by Stanley Hauerwas and Samuel Wells, 360-74. Malden, Mass: Blackwell Publishing, 2006.

Schultze, Quentin. *Here I Am: Now What on Earth Should I Be Doing*. Grand Rapids, Mich: Baker Books, 2005.

Shenk, Sara Wenger. *Anabaptist Ways of Knowing*. Telford, Pa: Cascadia Publishing House, 2003.

Simons, Menno. *The Complete Writings of Menno Simons*, trans. Leonard Verduin. Scottdale, Pa: Herald Press, 1956; reprint, 1978.

Snyder, C. Arnold. *Following in the Footsteps of Christ*. Maryknoll, NY: Orbis Books, 2004.

"Some Stories from Soldiers Who Became Conscientious Objectors," *MCC Peace Office Newsletter* (January-March 2008): 8

Sowinski, Greg. "Chavalia Claims Self-Defense," *The Lima News* (August 1, 2008): A7.

Stutzman, Paul. *Hiking Through: Finding Peace and Freedom on the Appalachian Trail*. Austin,Tex: Synergy Books, 2009.

Tanner, Kathryn. *Economy of Grace*. Minneapolis: Fortress Press, 2005.

Thomas, Edwina. "Can These Bones Live," *SOMA (Sharing of Ministries Abroad) Newsletter*. (October 15, 1996): 1-15.

Villegas, Isaac. "A Fugitive Church," *The Mennonite* (September 16, 2008): 2.

Vogt, Virgil. *The Christian Calling*. Scottdale, Pa: Mennonite Publishing House, 1961.

Weaver, Alain Epp. *States of Exile*. Scottdale, Pa: Herald Press, 2008

Weaver, J. Denny. "The Socially Active Community: An Alternative Ecclesiology," in *The Limits of Perfection: A Conversation with J. Lawrence Burkholder*, edited by Rodney Sawatsky and Scott Holland, 70-94. Waterloo, Ont: Conrad Grebel College.

Weaver, J. Denny and Gerald Biesecker-Mast, *Teaching Peace: Nonviolence and the Liberal Arts*. Lanham, Md : Rowman and Littlefield, 2003.

Wells, Samuel. *Improvisation: The Drama of Christian Ethics*. Grand Rapids, Mich: Brazos Press, 2004.

Whitman, Walt. *Leaves of Grass*. New York: Modern Library, n.d.

Williams, Rowan. *Why Study the Past? The Quest for the Historical Church*. Grand Rapids, Mich: William B. Eerdmans Publishing Company, 2005.

Willimon, William. "Repent," in *Bread and Wine: Readings for Lent and Easter*. Maryknoll, NY: Orbis Books, 2005.

Yoder, John Howard. "Armaments and Eschatology." *Studies in Christian Ethics* 1 (1988): 43-61.

Yoder, John Howard. *Body Politics: Five Practices of the Christian Community before the Watching World*. Scottdale, Pa: Herald Press, 2001.

Yoder, John Howard. *The Fullness of Christ: Paul's Revolutionary Vision of Universal Ministry*. Elgin, Ill: Brethren Press, 1987.

Yoder, John Howard, ed., *The Legacy of Michael Sattler*. Scottdale, Pa: Herald Press, 1973.

Yoder, John Howard. *The Politics of Jesus*. Grand Rapids, Mich: Eerdmans, 1994.

Yoder, John Howard. *The Priestly Kingdom*. South Bend, Ind: University of Notre Dame Press,1984.

Yoder, John Howard. *The Royal Priesthood*. Grand Rapids, Mich: Eerdmans, 1994.

York, Tripp. *The Purple Crown*. Scottdale, Pa: Herald Press, 2007.

Zijpp, N. van der. "Lysken Dirks," in *Mennonite Encyclopedia 3*, Scottdale, Pa: Herald Press, 1957.

Žižek, Slavoj. *The Fragile Absolute*. London: Verso, 2000.

Žižek, Slavoj. *The Parallax View*. Cambridge, Mass: MIT Press, 2006.

SCRIPTURE INDEX

SUBJECT INDEX

THE AUTHOR

Gerald J. Mast is professor of communication at Bluffton University. He is the author of *Separation and the Sword in Anabaptist Persuasion* (2006) and co-author, with J. Denny Weaver, of *Defenseless Christianity* (2009). He has also co-edited a number of volumes, including *Teaching Peace: Nonviolence and the Liberal Arts* (2003) and *The Work of Jesus Christ in Anabaptist Perspective* (2008). A  graduate of Malone College, he received a PhD in rhetoric and communication from the University of Pittsburgh.

Mast was born and raised in Holmes County, Ohio, with deep family roots in the Amish and conservative Mennonite communities. Throughout his life, he has remained affiliated with the Mennonite church and is a member of First Mennonite Church, Bluffton, Ohio. He currently is vice-chair of *The Mennonite* magazine board and editor of *Studies in Anabaptist and Mennonite History*.

Mast is married to Carrie (Roth) Mast and is the father of three young children: Anna, Jacob, and Jorian.